Discovering the Glorious Love of Christ

by John Durant
with chapters by C. Matthew McMahon

Copyright Information

Discovering the Glorious Love of Christ, by John Durant, with chapters by C. Matthew McMahon
Edited by Therese B. McMahon and Susan Ruth

Table of Contents

Lovesick for the Savior

by C. Matthew McMahon, Ph.D., Th.D.

Song of Songs 2:4-5, "He brought me into the banqueting house and his banner over me was love. Sustain me with cakes of raisins, refresh me with apples, for I am lovesick."

This *song* of songs is *divinely* inspired. It drips with the sweetness of the love of Christ for his spouse. The Holy Spirit thought it wise to add this wonderful song to the canon and rule of Scripture, for better understanding the love of the Messiah to his church. It is not simply a song about marital love. It is the song of *all* songs. A love between a husband and wife is infinitely *lacking* in comparison to the immeasurable love between Christ and *his* bride. The *entire song* is an argument for experimental Christian walking in light of the love of the Redeemer, Jesus Christ, to the soul of his people. It is an excellent mirror to demonstrate the manner in which *communion with God* takes place.

What is contained in this song? It sets out the love between Christ and the church, in the similitude of the depth of love between a husband and his beloved. It is a divine and heavenly love. But why *a song?* Why not a direct discourse? There are certain types of markers in Scripture that cause the exegete to take time to notice certain linguistical points. Wisdom literature (Proverbs), apocalyptic literature (Revelation), poetry

(Job), and even, *poetry in song,* are "markers." And in looking at the whole scope of this song, even though written in the Old Testament, it *surely* expresses the Gospel, and the realities surrounding the walk of believers to the Lord Jesus in extravagant love. The Song of Songs echoes Psalm 45, the wedding Psalm, which is a shorter version of the theme of the promised Messiah and God's church. Be reminded, Jesus said to the Pharisees, "You search the Scriptures, for in them you think you have eternal life; and these are they which *testify of me,"* (John 5:39). This song *testifies* of Christ. With that said, what is the depth of Song 2:5? I can tell you at the outset, it *passes knowledge.*

Christ has *brought* his people into his house. The text says, "He *brought* me into the banqueting house." No thieves shall break in and no man or woman comes of their own accord. They are *brought to a secure house.* What is the manner in which the church comes into feast with Christ? *He brought me,* from the Hebrew word meaning *to bring a thing.* God comes to his bride and ushers her into the banqueting hall, the *feast* of his house. He has promised to do it and he does it through the fulfillment of the Messiah Jesus Christ. It is the main motif of the song. *God* has brought this to pass. He has dominion over history, and such language, being "brought into his house," is used in the proclamation of salvation history. God's people are brought into his sanctuary in order to pray and bring sacrifices of praise for the salvation he gives them. God opened his arms of *extravagant love* and embraced his people for eternity through Jesus Christ. Where exactly does he bring them?

God brings his people into his house – *bayit* – a house of feasting. It is the house of *God's* feast. The idea of the banquet used has connotations of the extravagance of the sacrificial drink offering. Literally, it is saying that he brings his people into *the house of wine*. The Hebrew idea means to pour out as on the sacrifices on the brazen altar in the temple, (Exod. 29:40). The extravagance of the wine as seen in Song 8:2[1] is made from spiced wine mixed with the expense of pomegranate juice. The very use of the word "wine" shows *the great expense* of God's feast of love. It does not give the picture of gluttony, but by way of the extravagant banqueting that God brings his people to feast on *his* sweetness.

God has taken his people from where they were, in *their* house, and brought them into *his* house. For all intents and purposes, from the outhouse of sin, like the prodigal in the pigsty, to God's house of feasting, or the father's house of celebration *with* the prodigal.[2] When the people of God enter this house and enter the banqueting and feasting on God in his extravagant love, they see a mantle. We see this is no ordinary house by the mantle. God's mantle states, "that his banner over me

---

[1] "I would cause thee to drink of spiced wine of the juice of my pomegranate," (Song 8:2).
[2] Or, also, the table prepared by God in Psalm 23 where cups overflow.

is love." The Hebrew rendering is more *adult* in its scope. "He covered me with his love." She eats of *his fruit*, she drinks *his wine*, she is *covered by his intimacy*. The word comes from the Hebrew to "look" or "behold." In Numbers 1:52 and 2:3 it refers to the stately standard or banner above their tents – their name inscribed for all to see. The meaning here is that God does not hide his love for her.

The banner of God for his people is *love*. The banner, standard or covering for his people is *love*. It is *extravagant love* in which he has an intimate affection for them. This is like an uncommon love. Here is found God's everlasting love for his people. "Because the LORD loves His people," (2 Chron. 2:11), and, "The LORD has appeared of old to me, saying: "Yes, I have loved you with an everlasting love; Therefore with lovingkindness I have drawn you," (Jer. 31:3). The only real drink that will be taken in at this banquet is love, and its very banner is *love*. The church is brought into a house of feasting *filled* with love. It is a transcendent love which motivated God to save. Not only does he bring the church into his banquet by love, but love, as Romans 5:8 tells us, was the motivation for his saving hand to bring his people him, and draw them into his house, to bring them in by Christ. He demonstrates this in love *through Christ*.

The bride's *malady* is also seen here in the text. She is *lovesick*. This is not a love-sickness because she does not have the presence or support of the Beloved. It is not a longing of absence. This is a love-sickness because she is in the *presence* of the Beloved. She looks to be set in the context of this feast of love, where she is love-sick with his presence, and she looks for the continued communion with her beloved in such a way that this love will never be appeased, but always filled, and never end.

The spouse is sustained by Christ's provision, a provision of loving-kindness. It is not enough to be brought in, but also that he feeds and sustains his people as well. It is not enough to give a poor man shelter, for he could die in the house. In the Hebrew culture it would have been rude of the host to bring guests into a house to fend for themselves. Rather, God feeds his people. Feed me – *sustain me*. It means leaning on him wholly. God sustains his people as they lean upon him in his house of love. It shows all the excellencies of the Lord Jesus Christ and all his provisions showered on the church in his extravagant love.

There is a note made on *what* she eats. Raisin cakes – a delicacy. She also eats apples – a pleasant odor, with a connotation of a *sweet aroma*. Again, these images are of expensive provision which point to his love for her. The bride does not eat *dinner*. She *feasts* and dines with Christ from Christ in his house under the banner of triumphant love. The eyes affect the heart; whatever she sees, her heart melts within her. Raisin cakes and apples both point towards the deliciousness of the feasting on him. God has made an expensive provision for his people; so expensive in that it cost the

Father his *dear Son*. They in turn feed on Christ; they feed on the word. Banqueting is done by feasting on the Word of God, which is feasting on the Christ.

Christ's people receive nourishment for their soul *from* the banquet. Being sustained and refreshed they in turn exemplify intense love. The banner over the church is love. The colors of the banner, the majestic visible depiction of communion, is love. Love, according to the Apostle Paul is the greatest thing. "But now abide faith, hope, love, these three; but the greatest of these is love," (1 Cor. 13:13). Love is chief, love is supreme, and God is moved by love for his people, and they are moved by love for him. Again, "But God demonstrates his own love toward us, in that while we were yet sinners, Christ died for us," (Rom. 5:8). And he brings them by way of love into his feast and banquet of the Word. The spouse, once and again, speaks of herself as overpowered with the love of Christ, so as to weaken her body, and make her faint.

As a result of this loving provision, that which God has done for his people, they in turn love him intensely. They are *lovesick* – sick at heart with love. They are lovesick down to their very core and very being. His presence and his love motion her to be sick with love in return. She is, in return for his love to her, in bringing her in, in ushering her into the feast, sick with love for him. She does not bring herself in, this is the job of the beloved to usher her into the feast. Such love-sickness would never be if it were her power and her work of coming to the house. She was brought in by love, now she is sick with it in the majesty and benevolence of his presence. The Beloved gives her unfettered access to all his benefits. He does this for the church, through the word of God.

We find that the extravagant love of Jesus Christ is the believer's support, provision and feast. How does one respond to the extravagant love of God? How do you respond to such a love if you are a believer?

When the banner of Christ's love covers the soul, the soul becomes sick in love with Christ. The sinner says of himself, *has the Lord God loved me, given the Savior for me, flooded me with more benefits than I know what to do with? How is God so merciful in Christ to me, it is beyond my understanding and it passes knowledge!* Such a love kindles in the soul a flame that burns for the presence of God to remain near. This is a *dwelling with God* and a *dwelling with Christ.* Those in the church are not ashamed to profess this. But unless they know what this is, they can never experience it as Christ desires them to. This is where John Durant will be a great help.

Durant, in this wonderful work on making a discovery of Christ's love to his people, is going to plumb the depths of Christ's *transcendent* love from Ephesians 3:19, where the Apostle says that Christ's love for his people, "passeth knowledge." What does Durant mean by this love being transcendent? He will show that Christ's love for his people is *preeminent and supreme,* lying *beyond* the ordinary range of perception. Can such a study be accomplished adequately, in light of Christ's infinite beneficence and benevolence to his people? Durant is a skilled watchman, and will show, in part, yet, in a most *vivid* description, the relationship between Christ and the believer in the love of Christ which passes knowledge. It makes believers "lovesick" as with the spouse to her Beloved.

Durant will take a course to outline and explain four main parts to his overall subject, and expound Ephesians 3:19, "And to know the love of Christ, which passeth knowledge, that ye might be filled with all the fulness of God." He will show how the love of Christ *passes knowledge* as it, 1. Includes the truth and reality of Christ's love to the saints. 2. As it concludes the height and royalty, or transcendency of that love. 3. As it holds out the apostle's desire that the Ephesians might know both. And, 4. As it contains the ground of keeping up the Ephesian's hearts from fainting at Paul's tribulations, which is the drift and scope that Paul strives for in them.

In exploring this transcendent love of Christ to the soul, he will show that Christ's love is the saint's *life*. In fact, even at the outset, Durant will observe from Scripture that the love of Christ for the believer, from the Beloved to his spouse, is *so high* that there is no reaching of it, so deep that there is no sounding of it, so long that it exceeds measuring, and so broad that there is no comprehending it. Yet, though it is so high, and so lovely, and infinite in its scope, believers are beckoned to strive to understand, to *apprehend* it, in its communication to their heart, soul and mind. In fact, when they have finished reading this work by Durant, if they have soaked in even a measure of what he explains, they will come away with being *lovesick* for the Savior.

In the immeasurable grace and love of the Redeemer,
C. Matthew McMahon, Ph.D., Th.D.
From my study, January, 2021
"...search the Scriptures..." (John 5:39).

Meet John Durant

by C. Matthew McMahon, Ph.D. Th.D.

John Durant (1620-1686) was a zealous and popular independent puritan preacher. He often preached at Sandwich in Kent (1644), but lived at Canterbury, where he gathered a separate church, and dispensed the word and ordinances of the gospel. His published works bear out Edmund Calamy's description of him as "an excellent practical preacher." They also show him to have been a man of some learning, acquainted with both Greek and Hebrew as well as Latin. After the *Restoration* he was ejected from Canterbury Cathedral, but of his further history nothing is known.

His works are:

1. *Comfort and Counsel for Dejected Soules.* Being the heads and sum of divers Sermons preached to a particular congregation, 1651, 4th ed. 1658, where the author is described as pastor of a church of Christ in Canterbury, i.e. the cathedral.

2. *Sips of Sweetness, or Consolation for weak Believers,* 1651.

3. *The Salvation of Saints by the Appearances of Christ Now in Heaven and Hereafter from Heaven,* 1653.

4. *A Discovery of Glorious Love, or the Love of Christ to Believers,* being the sum of 6 Sermons on Ephes. 3:19, preached at Sandwich eleven years before (1655).[3]

5. *The Spiritual Seaman, or a Manual for Mariners,* being a short tract comprehending the principal heads of Christian religion, handled in allusion to the Seaman's Compass and Observations, 1655; reissued, with alterations, as The Christian's Compass, 1658.

6. *Altum Silentium, or Silence the Duty of Saints under every sad Providence,* a Sermon preached after the death of a Daughter by her Father, 1659 (September).

---

[3] *A Discovery of Glorious Love, or, The Love of Christ to Believers Opened,* in the truth, transcendency, and sweetness thereof together with the necessity that lies upon every believer, to strive after the spiritual and experimental knowledge of it: being the sum of 6 sermons preached upon Ephesians 3:19, by John Durant, Preacher of the Gospel in the City of Canterbury. "We will make thy love to be remembered more than wine," Song of Songs 1:4, and "He brought me into the house of wine, & his banner over me was love," (Song of Songs 2:4), (London: 1655).

7. *A Cluster of Grapes taken out of the Basket of the Woman of Canaan,* being the Sum of certain Sermons, 1660.

Sermon 1

"And to know the love of Christ, which passes knowledge, that ye might be filled with all the fulness of God," (Eph. 3:19).

Knowledge is the perfection of the rational creature. It is that by which we come (as the philosopher speaks) to *partake* of divinity, to be like the deity. God is light, and is all knowing, all knowledge; and the more we partake of knowledge the more we are like him. And the more like God we are, the nearer we are to perfection.

Knowledge is exceedingly precious. It must necessarily be so, since it tends to perfection. Indeed, as Aquinas says of seeing, though the object of sight is common in and of itself, the very act of seeing is sweet. So, he determines this point of the idea of *knowing*. However lowly and poor the object of knowledge is, the very *act* of knowing is high and precious.

Now, of all knowledge there is none so precious, nor so perfecting, as that which is divine. Other knowledge (such as human knowledge) can make us perfect only as men. This divine knowledge gives us a perfection as *saints*. And of all divine knowledge, the knowledge of Jesus Christ in the light of love is the most precious, as tending most to the perfection of our souls.

As there are degrees of luster in the heavenly lights, so there are degrees of glory in divine truths.

Every star in the firmament has a glorious light, yet the light of the sun exceeds them all in glory. And every truth (which is as a star in the heaven of divinity) has a peculiar excellency in it, and its knowledge is precious. Moreover, Jesus Christ, who is as the sun in divinity's heaven, has a *transcendent* excellency in him. So, to know him is far more to the perfecting of our souls than the knowledge of all truths otherwise. Therefore, this is the knowledge which Paul accents with an excellency in Philippians 3:8, "Yea doubtless, I count all things but loss for the excellency of the knowledge of Christ Jesus my Lord." And certainly, Paul might well say this in this way. For although he had attained the knowledge of other things, yet apart from a knowledge of Christ he would have been at a loss, in regard to soul-sacred perfection. So that whatever other knowledge is in some way perfecting and precious, and therefore desirable, yet there is no knowledge which is so to be desired (at least by saints) as the knowledge of Jesus Christ.

Although the sun is the most glorious of the heavenly lights, mortals receive more comfort by its heat than by its light. In the same manner, though the knowledge of Jesus Christ is the most transcendent of divine truths, our souls receive more sweetness by the warmth of his love than by the luster of his light. Moses could not see the glory of God and live (and as a result must die) except that he saw *his grace.* In the same way, our souls cannot see the luster of the bright beams of Christ's glory and live (we must die so that we can behold that). Notwithstanding, we must see the light of the heart-love of Jesus, or else we will die. If this light does not dawn on our hearts, if this knowledge does not shine into our hearts, we shall sink and die in our souls, especially if we are in fear of any troubles.

In this epistle Paul shares many precious petitions which he sends up to the Father of our Lord Jesus on behalf of the Ephesians. And in our text, he adds that they might, "know the love of Christ which passes knowledge." I shall now briefly give you the context to help shed some light to the text.

Having hinted in the first verse of this chapter that he was a prisoner of Jesus Christ for the Ephesians (who were Gentiles) and having also spoken of the excellency of the gospel and the warrant which he had to preach the same to them (which two things were great supporters of him in his sufferings), the apostle comes in the 14th verse to pray for the Ephesians that they might not faint at his tribulations. Here are two reasons the apostle may have feared that the Ephesians might faint at the news of his tribulations.

1. They would likely feel sympathy. It is typical for saints to sympathize with each other in their tribulations. And Paul on this ground might rightly think that the tidings of his imprisonment would be sad to these Ephesians. He might fear that out of their tender love, both to his person and preaching, that they would be overly sad with sympathy when they hear that now their preacher was in prison.

2. They may also experience fear that they themselves might meet with the same sufferings. For what might they think? Is Paul in prison for preaching the gospel? Then we may rightly fear the same for receiving the gospel.

It is commonly seen that the receivers of gospel truths suffer as well as the revealers. And certainly (the Ephesians might say) we shall be accounted as guilty for believing the gospel as Paul is for preaching it. Perhaps they might argue, and fear, and despair. Therefore, the apostle bends his knees to the Father of our Lord Jesus, who alone is able to keep believers from faltering in the faith and support them when they lose heart. To that end, he asks the Lord for three things on their behalf, that they might not (on any ground) faint at his tribulations.

1. Divine strength. That he would grant "according to the riches of his glory, that they might be strengthened with might by his Spirit in the inner man," (verse 16). The apostle knew how weak the spirit of man is and how readily it can lose heart, unless God strengthens it. Therefore, he begs the Spirit of God (which is the power from on high) for their strengthening in the inner man, that they might not faint in their outward man.

2. Christ's inhabitation. "That Christ may dwell in your hearts by faith," (verse 17). If anything will keep the heart from fainting it is Christ's indwelling presence in the soul. Christ's presence creates comfort, and there

is no such fence against losing heart in the face of any fear as Christ in the soul. The inhabitation of Christ within will support the soul from despair at tribulation.

3. The knowledge of Christ's love. That they might, "know the love of Christ which passes knowledge," as it is in the text. Paul knew well the power and efficacy of Christ's love.

So now you may gather up the apostle's petitions into one prayer, and you may conceive him pouring out his heart after this manner: "Father of our Lord Jesus, since you are the God of all comforts, and comfort yours in all their tribulations so that they do not faint, promise to grant according to the riches of your grace that the Ephesians may not faint at my tribulations. And to this end, strengthen them by your Spirit of power in their inner man; fill them by the glorious presence of Christ dwelling in them; but above all, let them know the love of Jesus Christ which passes knowledge."

You see all this by the context, the drift and scope of the text. But before I speak any further to it, I must address one thing which may be an occasion of doubt, and that is the seeming unreasonableness of this part of Paul's prayer. For some may say, what reason should Paul pray for that which he hints is impossible? Why should he pray that the Ephesians might know that which he expressly says is above knowledge: the love of Christ which *passes knowledge?*

There are three things which may satisfy this concern as well as demonstrate the reasonableness of this request.

1. I admit that the love of Christ is above knowledge, yet it is not unreasonable to desire to know it. The fulfilling of divine precepts is above our power, and yet it is to be our endeavor. In the same manner, although the knowledge of Christ and his love is above our intellectual capacities, it should still be in our desires. The same infiniteness, which grace puts in the will, causes us to endeavor to pursue what we cannot attain perfectly. This grace instills in us a desire for the obtaining of that which cannot be obtained.

2. To know the love of Christ may be said to be above knowledge with reference to men as men, though not to saints as such. Indeed, the spirit of man is not able to know or search into the love of Christ, as that is above knowing. But the Spirit of Christ is able both to search into and to reveal his love. And though Christians as men cannot attain to the knowledge of the love of Christ by the light of reason, yet as saints by the light of faith they may, especially with the Holy Spirit "shedding it abroad" in their hearts, as Romans 5:5 states.

3. The love of Christ may be said to be above knowledge in regard to perfection of degrees, not simply in regard to its parts. It is true, the perfect knowledge of Christ's love passes the understanding of men and angels (which is its glory). Yet in some measure it may be known (and it is our duty to know). For that which

cannot be known perfectly in the highest degree may yet be known partially and in some measure.

In this way the text may be cleared from the doubt propounded.

Now, there are four ways in which I shall look on this scripture, and so speak to it.

1. As it includes the truth and reality of Christ's love to the saints.

2. As it concludes the height and royalty, or transcendency of that love.

3. As it holds out the apostle's desire that the Ephesians might know both.

4. As it contains the ground of keeping up the Ephesian's hearts from fainting at Paul's tribulations, which is the drift and scope that Paul strives for in them.

And in this way, there will be four doctrines which I shall take up and speak to from these words.

1. There is love in Christ's heart towards all believers.

2. That love which Christ bears to believers is a transcendent love.

3. It is a thing of necessary concern for every Christian to know the transcendent love of Christ.

4. The spiritual knowledge of the transcendent love of Christ towards believers is of special efficacy to keep their hearts from fainting under any trouble.

I begin with the first, which might more fully be gathered from another text, yet because it will be a good foundation for the following discourse and is clear enough in this place, I shall briefly speak to it now, *viz.* there is love in Christ's heart towards all believers.

I suppose this is evident in these words. Paul would not pray that the Ephesians might know that which was not; things must exist so they can be *known*. Nothing falls under the understanding until it first is something in being. I shall briefly open the point, and then prove it and apply it.

How love may be said to be in Christ (as any other affection) I shall not need to inquire. And yet love may be said to be in Christ as he is God in a far more proper sense than any other passion may, because it is his essence, God being love (1 John 4:16).

I shall not attempt to define what the love of Christ is. The moralists have so many definitions of love that indeed it is hard to know what it is among their various definitions. Bypassing their niceties, however, I shall content myself with this plain description of love. *Love is the commanding affection of the soul, consisting in the expansion of the heart as it moves towards a person or thing in hopes and workings for its good.*

I call it an affection, and it is a commanding one. Love is the queen regent in the soul, and it sits on the throne commanding everything. It is the centurion in the heart and has the same power over all the affections as the centurion has over all his servants.

It consists in the expansion or stretching out of the heart. As hatred contracts and pulls inward, so love opens and dilates the heart. I add that it consists (in general) in hopes and workings for good. I do not specify the end, for that describes and denominates the particular kinds of love; therefore, only in general do I say it consists in an expansion of the heart in wishing and working for the good of the person or thing loved.

So that now, when I say that there is love in Christ's heart towards all believers, I mean that the commanding affections of Jesus Christ are set on them, that his heart is open and stretched out to them, and that the hopes and workings of his soul are toward them for their good.

By *believers*, in a word, understand that I am referring to all those who *close* with Christ as tendered in the gospel. However, there are differences between believers in the degrees of their faith and the ways of their light, yet all agreeing in this, that they see themselves lost without Christ, and that God the Father freely tenders Jesus in the word of grace to them. They then move toward him in the strength and sincerity of their souls to embrace him as he is tendered. They are believers, all of them, who do this. Once this is done, Christ places no difference (as it is in Acts 15:9)[4] between them, but burns in his heart with real love toward them all.

For proof, I should bring all that cloud of witnesses which would gladly come and set a seal to this sweet truth. Ask John, and he will witness that *Christ loved him*. He was indeed a heart-beloved believer; and

---

[4] "And put no difference between us and them," (Acts 15:9).

of him it is often said that he was "the disciple whom Jesus loved." Yes, and John will witness for more than himself, he says Jesus loved him and all believers besides him. For speaking to them, Christ says he, "hath loved us," (Rev. 1:5). Call in Paul, and he will prove that Christ loves believers, for Christ loved *him*. And such was the love that Christ demonstrated to Paul that he professes that he could, no, *did* live on it. "I live," he says, "by the Son of God who loves me," (Gal. 2:20). Paul further bears record to this truth and witnesses that Christ's love stretches forth itself to every believing soul, as we are, "more than conquerors, through him that loves us," (Rom. 8:37). I will add no more testimonies to prove this truth. Even the least believer, though but a babe, is able to lisp in the language of this love and tell you that there is a divine fire of love in Christ's heart, burning brightly towards believers.

I shall now mention three demonstrations of the doctrine taken from the behavior of Christ towards believers, which will clear the idea of this cordial love to them.

1. Christ's eye is always on believers, and he takes delight to look there where they are. The eye is the index of love. It is a sweet star always shining over the hearts and houses of those whom we love. The proverb tells us that *where we love, there we look*. Observe that Christ's eyes are *towards* believers. Will you listen to Christ's love in its language? "Let me see thy countenance," he says to the believer, "for it is lovely," (Song of Songs 2:14).

Such is the pleasure that Christ takes in beholding believers that he seems to live on their looks and speaks as if he were ravished with their sight. "Thou hast ravished my heart, my sister, my spouse, thou hast ravished my heart with one of thine eyes," (Song of Songs 4:9). He echoes, as if he sucked sweetness from the words, that, "you have ravished my heart," with your sight. How can we question Christ's love to believers when his eyes are fixed on them to such a degree that their sight ravishes his soul? Rest in this, O believing soul! Christ's delight in looking on you demonstrates his love to you. He peeps through the lattices to declare his love (Song of Songs 2:9). It is as if he were overwhelmed (as indeed such an effect produces such a look of love) while he beholds believers, for he says, "turn away thine eyes from me, for they have overcome me," (Song of Songs 6:5). The word signifies, "have made me proud," or as our marginal notes have it, "have puffed me up." Christ seems to pride himself in the looks of believers. His eye is on them and his heart is taken with them if their eye is on him.

2. Christ's tongue speaks his love to believers. The tongue is love's trumpet; the breathings of the heart fill the lips with sounds of love. Love that is secret in the heart sounds sweetly in the breath. Words as a silver trumpet loudly sounds love. It is said of Shechem, the son of Hamor, that his soul clave unto Dinah the daughter of Jacob, and the text says, "he loved her, and his tongue spoke it," and further, "that he spoke kindly

to the damsel," (Gen. 34:31). Believers, Christ's tongue reveals his heart. His lips speak his love to you. How often has Christ spoke sweetly to your soul? O believer! Can you not tell by his speaking what is in his heart? How near your heart do those words of your Savior go? "If any thirst, let him come and drink freely." Does not his heart open as a fountain of love in these words? He speaks so kindly when he says, "if you thirst, come and drink." Ask the poor woman that had the bloody issue in Mark chapter 5. Did not Christ speak to her in the language of love when he said, "daughter, your faith has made you whole?" She had touched him, maybe even before she was truly aware of it. So when he mentions it, she trembles, as if expecting a rebuke. But while she touched his garment secretly, love touched his heart sweetly and his tongue revealed it when he called her "daughter." And as Christ's tongue trumpets out love when he speaks of believers, consider the high epitaphs that he adds to believers' names when he speaks of their persons! Consider his language of love when he speaks of his spouse, "thou art fair," he says, "thou art fair, thou hast doves eyes; thy hair is as a flock of goats, thy teeth are like a flock of sheep; thy lips are like a thread of scarlet, thy neck like the tower of David," (Song of Songs 4:1-4). As believers declare their love to Christ by speaking highly of him, so Christ declares his love to believers by speaking highly of them. If believers call him the Lily of the Valley, he calls them the *lily* among thorns. Christ's love will not permit him to speak of them in base language. In this way the lips of your Lord, O believers, are a demonstration of his love to you.

3. Christ's actions seal this truth and strengthen the demonstration of the doctrine. If there were nothing but the eye or the tongue, it might be feared that the love expressed by them was either insincere or fond. But actions that back them up, seal the truth and prove that his love is not complemental but cordial. If love is only in the lips, it is without life and may be suspected as counterfeit. But when men not only speak but act love, then love lives and is demonstrated to be love indeed. Where love is in truth, it will be seen in act. Now we take a view of the actions of Jesus Christ, where we see that they strive to excel and exceed his words in the declaration of his love to believers. I shall only hint at some, as intending the larger discourse of them in the next doctrine.

1. Consider how Jesus Christ manifests himself and his secrets to believing souls, which demonstrates the truth of his love. Delilah questions the truth of Samson's love because he concealed his secrets from her, "how canst thou say, 'I love thee,' when thy heart is not with me?" (Judges 16:15). She argues that where there is love in truth, there will be a communication of secrets. "But this I do not find in you; therefore, I question whether you indeed love me." Regardless of the grounds Delilah argued this point against her Samson, believers cannot argue so against their Savior's love. The Lord Jesus unveiled himself to believers; the secrets of his

heart are with them. Christ tells his disciples that he would manifest himself to them (John 14). The men of the world are strangers to Christ's affections, and so to his secrets. Carnal people do not know the mind of the Lord because he does not love them. But we, Paul says, we who are beloved by Christ have the mind of Christ (1 Cor. 2:16). As the Father loves the Son and declares it by this, that he shows him all things which he does (John 5:10), in like manner the Son loves believers and actually demonstrates it by declaring all things, (*i.e.,* all these secrets which were needful for them to know), that he heard of the Father (John 15:15). The secrets of Christ's cabinet-counsel are with those whom he loves.

2. Christ often takes believers to his house and feasts with them. This is how we deal with our friends, and thus we declare to them our love. And this is how Christ deals with his, "the king has brought me into his chamber," (Song of Songs 1:4). "Nay he has brought me into his banqueting house," (Song of Songs 2:4). When David would declare his love to Barzillai, he said, "come you with me, and I will have you feed with me at Jerusalem," (2 Sam. 19:33). Christ often speaks in this way to declare his love to believers, "come thou to me, poor soul, and I will feed thee with me in Jerusalem." Christ declares his love not only by inviting and bringing believers to his house, but also by coming to theirs; he stands at their door and knocks, and if they will only open, he will enter (Rev. 3:20). If they love him so much as to let him in, he will come and declare his love by

dwelling with them (John 14:23), and he will feast with them in their house, *i.e.* in their hearts. And because he comes to show his love, he will prepare the feast at his own cost. "He has gathered his myrrh with his spice," for this purpose (Song of Songs 5:1).

3. Christ unites himself to believers, and by doing so demonstrates that he loves them. Affection begets union. Augustine defined love to be the juncture of two in one: *amor est junctura duo copulans,* love makes one of two. It is said of Jonathan and David that their souls were knit together (1 Sam. 18:1). Christ and believers are knit together, and it is Christ's love which makes the knot. It is more than a moral union between Christ and believers. They are not only his friends and brethren, but his spouses and members. If he is the head, they are the body; and if he is the vine, they are the branches. The union between Christ and believers is nearer than that of the vine and branches even, for no branch can be said to be in the vine, and the vine in it. But of believers it is said, Christ is in them, and they are in him. This union demonstrates the truth of Christ's love to believing souls. I shall now make a word of application, and then conclude this point. There are three uses about which I will speak, *viz.* a use of information, comfort, and counsel.

Use 1. The point informs us of the sweetness of Christ to all the saints. O how sweet, how kind, how gracious Jesus Christ is to believers, to consider them and to set his heart on them! Believers, the Lord loves you, is he not then sweet to you? At the consideration of Boaz's love, Ruth falls on her face and says, "why have I found grace in thine eyes, that thou shouldest take knowledge of me, seeing I am a stranger?" Fall on your faces believers! You were once strangers to Jesus Christ, but you have found grace in his eyes; your names are written on his heart in letters of love. Well may you say that Christ is sweet, seeing he loves such strangers as you were. The King of Israel is surely sweet in setting his love on you, who were strangers to Israel. O how happy are you, poor believer, in being the object of the Lord's love! The lowliest believer may raise up a very high structure of happiness upon the corner stone of Christ's love. O how blessed you are in your beloved, and how sweet he is to you! For he has a fire of love burning in his heart forever towards you!

Use 2. It is very comforting to believers that Christ loves you! Does it not revive your hearts, my brethren, to hear that he who is the Lord of life and glory in himself, is a Lord of grace and love to you? Jesus Christ who has written on his garments, "Lord of Lords," has also written upon his heart his love to his own. If you can only see how near you are to Christ, how highly he prizes you, how dearly he loves you, I should not need to bid you rejoice, or be glad, or be of good comfort.

Objection: If only I could see that Christ loved me, but I doubt it otherwise.

Answer: Do not doubt it (O believing soul) but be confident, and in that confidence be comforted:

Christ loves you, and that (as we shall show afterwards) with a transcendent love.

Objection: But, it is good to have a ground of confidence. I'm comforted in vain if I see no foundation for your words. What reason is there that Christ should love me?

Answer: Christ's love is its own reason. He therefore loves because *he will.* It may be the vanity of our earthly love that we love merely because *we* love. But it is the glory of Christ's love that he does so. The reason Christ loves you is because it is in his own heart to do so. If you look in your heart, you will not find it (because it is not there). But look into Christ's heart, and there it is. He will have mercy on whom he will. Christ will love you, and does love you, O believer, because he will. Do not therefore stand questioning *why* he should, but be comforted, and rejoice in this, that he does love you, even you, O poor soul. Though your faith may be small, yet Christ's love to you is true.

Question: But though he loves me now, will he love me still? Will not Christ dislike me hereafter, and upon that dislike desert me? Surely, I shall in time give him cause, and I fear he will take it. And certainly, if Christ deserts me, I will die. I cannot live without his love.

Answer: Neither die, nor doubt, poor soul! The Lord so loves you that he will not leave you. Or if he does for a time, he will not always. Christ's bowels burn with love, and that fire, however smothered for a time, will break out in a flame at last. Christ's love is like himself, immutable and unchangeable. Love is Christ's life. He will not surely kill himself by deserting you. You cannot live without Christ's love, and Christ cannot but love you, for he has sworn that the mountains shall be removed before his love for you ceases.

Objection: But though Christ loves me, yet men hate me. I cannot be so cheerful in Christ's love because I meet with the wrath of my fellow man.

Answer: I pity you, poor creature, because you have the love of the Potter, and yet you fear the wrath of the potsherd. Why are you so weak as to sink under the creature's wrath while you have the love of the Creator? Be of good comfort, Christ can break in pieces all your enemies with his iron rod, while in the meantime he will comfort you with his Shepherd's crook. Why do you droop at the hatred of him who dwells in a tabernacle of clay instead of triumphing in the love of him who is set down at the right hand of the Majesty on high? Look up believer, heaven is clear over your head though the earth is dirty under your feet. Though you are in a storm among the creatures, yet the sun of love shines on you from Christ. He smiles down at you and loves you, so what if men hate you? Do not fear him who hates your body, and at worst can only destroy that. Rejoice rather in him who loves your soul, and at the last will raise up your body from the grave and give you a glorious body like his own and fill your soul with eternal joy in the enjoyment of his everlasting love.

The last use of the point is for counsel. As Christ loves his saints, I would counsel both the world and believers.

First, you men of the world, if you have an ear to hear, hear. Christ loves believers, and so should you. Certainly, Christ will take it well at your hands, if you love those who are beloved by him. His friends are sometimes strangers in your land. Use them well, show them love, and attribute it to Christ's score. He loves them, and he will reward you for doing likewise. Jesus Christ so loves believers that he will not let a cup of cold water given to them in his name (that is, because he loves them) go unrewarded. I say it again, seeing as Christ is gracious and loves believers, you would be wise to love them also. However, take heed that you do not wrong them. If you will not do them good, beware that you do them no harm. For if you do, Christ will not bear it. Tremble, unless while you lift up your hand against believers, that Jesus Christ who loves them, dash you in pieces. Beware of persecuting Christ's beloved ones under pretenses. It will be a poor excuse at best to say they were troublemakers, for Christ knows them to be saints. The blood of believers is very precious to him, and he will punish all those who dare touch believers under any pretense. Therefore, if you will not be so wise as to love, I warn you to not be so mad as to hurt those whom Christ loves.

But secondly, let this counsel believers, that since the Lord Jesus loves them so, they should walk worthy of his love. Believers, live as the objects of Christ's love. Advance his kingdom, embrace his counsels, love all his members, be abundant in his work and service. In all things show that Christ's love to you has a constraining power in you. At least be counseled to love Christ, who loves you and who therefore deserves your love, though you do not deserve his. O! do not let the love of Christ plead against you and say, "I ran out to them, but they returned not unto me." Do not let Christ say, "I gave you counsel, and you rejected it; in love I gave you commandments, and you transgressed them." Seeing as Christ loves you, love him; and if you love him, keep his commandments. Rouse up yourselves, O believing souls! Considering that Christ loves you, submit yourselves accordingly. If he calls, come. If he bids you go, go. If his kingdom is advancing, join in the work, for it is his kingdom of him that loves you. If his Spirit counsels you, accept it, for it comes from love. In a word, in all things live as those who indeed are beloved of Christ. And let your carriage be obedient, kind, and loving to him who stoops so low as to love such poor creatures as you and me. And if any ask why you love and labor for Jesus Christ, tell them, it is because you love him. Then add that if they only knew how much Christ loves you, they would ask instead, "why then do you love him so little, or not do more for him?" But if they demand, how does Christ love you? Tell them that question is unanswerable. Indeed say, he loves you truly and transcendently. Tell all the world how he loves you, tell them that his love surpasses your knowledge and understanding, for it is a love that is beyond knowledge.

Sermon 2

"And to know the love of Christ, which passes knowledge, that you might be filled with all the fulness of God," (Eph. 3:19).

Christ's love is the saint's life. Paul tells us that he was *dead to the law* that he might live to God. And the ground for this is that he lived by faith in Christ who *loved* him (Gal. 2:20). As the life, so likewise the comfort of the saints is wrapped up in the love of Christ. A believer can neither live, nor rejoice, if the Lord Jesus does not smile on his soul. But if Jesus Christ will but smile, and shine in the light of love, believers do not know only how to live, but also how to rejoice in even the worst of times. This is why the apostle is praying to the Father of our Lord Jesus for the Ephesians, that they might not faint at his tribulations, and he intreats the Father that they may know the love of Christ which passes knowledge.

Having briefly touched on the reality of Christ's love to believers, I shall now speak to the *royalty* of this love that passes knowledge, this transcendent love.

You can see how fully this point is evident in these words. It must necessarily be transcendent, since the apostle says, *it passes knowledge.*

I shall endeavor to open the point, and give you its meaning, by bringing you to the top of this hyperbolical expression in three steps or stairs.

First, the love of Christ to believers is transcendent because it is *above expression*. Those who enjoy Christ's love do not know how to express it. Such is the nature of transcendent love, that it is beyond their knowledge of how to express it in any language. The Scripture describes high and majestic aspects of God as being unspeakable. So, when it would elevate and declare the transcendency of that rapture which Paul experienced when he was taken up to the third heaven, it is described as unutterable and unspeakable, impossible for any man to express (2 Cor. 12:14). The Scripture also speaks of the transcendent and "unspeakable" joy Christians experience by believing in 1 Peter 1:8, "You rejoice with joy unspeakable."

It must not be passed by in silence, that the joy of which Peter speaks is that which believers have by faith, a joy that is certainly founded on Christ's love. And if the joy in the faith of Christ's love is unspeakable, the love itself is much more. For that which makes anything what it is must, by necessity, be at least that and much more itself. The first step to ascend to the height of the expression and to declare the transcendency of Christ's love that passes knowledge is this, that no man knows how to express it.

2. Christ's love is transcendent and may be said to be above knowledge in that it is above apprehension. Believer's language cannot express, nor can their knowledge apprehend, the height of their Savior's love. Men can often apprehend more than they can express;

even when the tongue is silenced, the understanding may still be comprehensive. But the love of Christ confounds the most intelligent of men and angels. It is so high that there is no reaching of it, so deep that there is no sounding of it, so long that it exceeds measuring, and so broad that there is no comprehending it. The most spiritual mathematician is not able to commensurate Christ's love in all its dimensions. It is as possible for that little crevasse of the body (the eye) to let in all the light of the sun, as it is for that great eye of the soul (knowledge) to let in the luster of Christ's love. The Holy Spirit describes transcendent as something that cannot be comprehended. For example, it is said that God does such great things that they are *beyond our understanding* (Job 37:5). Without a doubt, both the operations of the Father's hand and the expansion of the Son's heart are acts that cannot be comprehended. Likewise, both the Father's works and the Son's love equally transcend knowledge and are unable to be apprehended.

3. Christ bears to believers a transcendent love that passes knowledge in that it is above conception. Imagination can conceive that which reason cannot comprehend. Understanding that is bounded by reason cannot go beyond its limits; and therefore, where reason cannot suggest, the understanding cannot apprehend. But when imagination is given wings, it will fly to transcendent heights that reason cannot reach. Yet such, my beloved, is the love of Christ. It is so high, so

superlatively transcendent, that let imagination loose, and it will fly as high as it can. Still, it is not able to soar to the top. As understanding goes to its utmost bounds, so imagination flying beyond all bounds is still unable to conceive the love of Christ for believers.

So that now when I say the love which Christ bears to believers is transcendent, and when you read in the text that it *passes knowledge*, you may understand that it is above the expression of the finest oratory, the comprehension of the deepest theory, and the conception of the most sublime imagination. Let oratory speak, wisdom study, imagination fly, and yet neither the one, nor the other, nor all, can express, apprehend, or conceive the love of Christ to believers. Indeed, the love of Christ is such as heaven itself does not exalt the saints so high as to make them able to comprehend that love. As it is with fish in the sea, they swim up and down the mighty waters, but they do not, and cannot, comprehend that watery world in which they live. In like manner, the saints above swim up and down the infinite ocean of love, (which is in their Savior's heart), and yet they can no more comprehend that vast sea of love in which through eternity they shall bathe and bless their souls than the little fish can comprehend the great sea in which it swims. Therefore, before I proceed further, let me premise that it is not in my thoughts, nor dare I presume, and neither would I have you expect, that by anything I shall or can say, I shall be able to set out the infiniteness of that love according to its full latitude and worth. No, it is this I despair of. And yet I desire to let you see some of the glimmering beams of the transcendent love in Christ's heart toward believers so that you may wonder at it and study it. And as a painter when he intends to draw out the sea or the world in a map, he makes only some little shadows of the earth and sea that so the beholder may be able to guess at its vastness. In the same manner I shall draw before you in my discourse some little shadowy lines of Christ's love, that in so doing I may help you imagine what is that infinite transcendent love, which neither saints nor angels are able (in all its luster and dimensions) to paint out or discover.

For proof, I shall not need to add more Scripture, as it is clear enough by what the apostle says in our text about Christ's love, that it is transcendent. In the verse before this, the apostle hints that there are vast and infinite dimensions of Christ's love; it has breadth, and length, and depth, and height. And it is worth noting that the apostle does not tell how great those dimensions are; he does not say how broad, or how long, or how deep, or how high. But rather, it is as if the dimensions of Christ's love transcend understanding, and only adds this, that this love passes knowledge.

To my remembrance, this phrase is only found once more in the New Testament in Philippians 4:7. Here Paul says, speaking of the transcendency of the peace of God, that it "passes understanding." Certainly, it is the glory of Christ's love, as well as of his Father's peace, that it also passes understanding.

If you read and spiritually consider what is presented in the Song of Songs, you will see that the love of Christ to believers is transcendent in its glory, convincing power, and proof. You may have wondered at some strange stories of love which you have heard or read about in the past. But alas! If you attempt to compare the highest love story you ever heard about with the love of Christ to believers, you will be forced to confess that such a love, in comparison, is a mere whim. If ever strength of affection was demonstrated in sweetness of expression, it is to be found in the Song of Songs. When I consider the fourth chapter of that song, I cannot help but wonder at the high transcendency of Christ's love to believers. Most assuredly I conclude that the affections are sweet, strong, glorious, and inconceivable when the expressions are so *ravishing*, so great, so high, as they are in that chapter.

I shall give one general demonstration to let you see that Christ's love to believers is transcendent, and this is shown in the true nature of his love which comprehends all kinds, acts, or demonstrations of love whatsoever. As such, it must be a transcendent love.

If there is some doubt about whether Christ's love to believers includes and contains in it all other kinds or acts of love, I will answer by an induction, or enumeration of the several kinds of love.

Among others, the moralists tell us of these four kinds of love: 1. A love of friendship, 2. A love of pity, 3. A love of sympathy, and, 4. A love of complacency.

Instead, I refer to these as four demonstrations, or degrees of one and the same passion of love rather than four kinds that are distinct and different. Further, I show that Christ's love to believers includes and contains all of them, and for this reason it must necessarily be transcendent.

1. The love of friendship is so called because it is that kind, or act, of love by which we follow one whom we see and love as a friend; and to whom we wish good. Now this kind (or degree) of love is found in the love of Christ to believers. Christ looks on and loves all believers as *friends*. He counts them as friends and calls them all by that name (John 15:14), and this truth appears in his dealing with them. "Henceforth I call you not servants; for the servant knows not what his Lord does. But I have called you friends; for all things that I have heard of the Father, I have made known unto you," (verse 15). Those whom we love as friends we open our minds to; we communicate the secrets of our heart to. Christ deals thus with believers, and thus dealing, does he not declare to them the love of friendship?

2. The love of pity. This follows on the former, for as Job says, to him that is afflicted pity should be showed by his friend (Job 6:14). This is included in Christ's love to believers. For upon that love of friendship which he bears to them, he shows pity toward them. When no eye

pitied them, his eye did. When sinners and Satan laugh at their misery, Christ sighs to see their sorrows and pities their souls. It is here said in Isaiah 63:9, "in his love, and in his pity he redeemed them, and he bare them, and carried them all the days of old."

3. The love of sympathy (which in truth is but a high degree of pity) is also contained in the love of Christ to believers. Men sympathize with those whom they love; they take up the miseries of their beloved on themselves. When Jesus Christ sees any believer groan under sin or sadness, he comes, and by a sympathy afflicts himself. "For in all their afflictions," the prophet says, "he was afflicted," (Isaiah 63:9), as if he himself was in their sadness and under their sin. The author to the Hebrews tells us, "we have not a high priest who cannot sympathize with our infirmities," (Heb. 4:15). His meaning is that indeed, our high priest, Jesus Christ, sympathizes with believers in their sorrows. And in Hebrews 5:2 it is said of Christ that he can have compassion for the ignorant. That word in the text signifies that he knows how to pity according to the measure of our misery. The misery can never be so great that Jesus Christ cannot measure out as great a measure of sympathy as is needful. In this you can see that Christ's love to believers contains in it also the love of sympathy.

4. The love of complacency (which indeed is the highest degree of love) is also contained in Christ's love to believers. You have a description of this love of

complacency (and a demonstration also of the thing in hand) in Zephaniah 3:17, "The Lord thy God who is in the midst of thee is mighty, he will save, he will rejoice over thee with joy. He will rest in his love; he will joy over thee with singing." It is the nature of the love of complacency to rest in itself and to rejoice in the object of its desire with singing. In this way Christ acts to believers. He first loves them, and then rests in that love. And after, he solaces himself in their souls and rejoices with singing while he rests in his love for them, over them, and in them. As the Father did from all eternity by his love of complacency, resting in the Son, and taking his delight in him (Proverbs 8:30). So does Jesus Christ rest in believers and solaces himself in their persons. For as it is there added in verse 31, "His delights were in the sons of men." In this way, Christ's love to believers is comprehended in this highest kind (or degree) of love, namely, that of complacency.

To summarize this demonstration, look how the sea transcends all other rivers, because they all come and empty themselves into it. In the same manner, the love of Christ excels all loves no matter what they are, and is transcendent; in as much as all the kinds, acts, or degrees of love which run up and down among the creatures do all meet and empty themselves in Christ's heart as into the vast ocean of love, and from there flows forth into the hearts of believers as the sole choice of this great, high, transcendent love.

To further discover the transcendency of Christ's love to believers, I shall now speak to it more particularly. And at this time, I shall touch on the substance and circumstances of this love, and in both, show how it transcends and passes all knowledge.

On the substance of the love of Christ to believers, when spiritually considered, it will appear to be transcendent. There are four things which I shall touch upon briefly, as the substantial declarations of the hyperbolic excellency of this love, namely, 1) the nature, 2) the degrees, 3) the duration, and 4) the operation of this love.

1. To begin with, the nature of Christ's love to believers is transcendent because it is of the same nature that the Father's is to him. Jesus Christ loves believers with the same kind, or nature of love, with which the Father loves himself. His love to them, and his Father's love to him, by nature are all one. And if there is transcendency in the one, (namely the Father's love to Christ) there must necessarily be also in the other (that is, Christ's love to believers) for they are in their nature both one and the same. Christ himself bears record to this truth. "As the Father has loved me, so I have loved you," (John 15:9). That you may fully feel the weight of this demonstration, take it in these three conclusions briefly.

1.) The most transcendent love of all is in God. For "God is love," (1 John 4:16). Water in the fountain is the sweetest, and love, in like manner, in God is clearest, for he is the God of love (2 Cor. 13:11). As light in the sun is the most transcendent, so the love of God must necessarily transcend, because love is in him, as light is in the sun, *i.e.* in its *primo*, and proper orb or seat. And indeed, as every beam of light is but the irradiation of the sun, so all the love which is in the hearts of creatures is like drops of dew which first fell from the heaven of love, God's heart.

2.) Of all the love which is in God, the most transcendent is that which he lets out to Christ. Christ is crowned with the flower, beauty, and glory of the Father's love. Jesus Christ was and is still, not only the Beloved but the Well-Beloved of the Father. The Father bestows the highest degree of his love on Christ, in whom he was well pleased. God's transcendent love for Christ is apparent in all his actions toward him. He made all things for him, he gave all things to him, and he does not allow so much as a drop of love to any creature, but that it first runs into his heart, and so through him to the creature. The very spirit and quintessence of that love which is in God's heart was let out, and that without measure, into Christ's.

3.) That love which Christ bears to believers is the same which he had from the Father. As it flowed from the Father's heart into his, so it flows from his heart into believers. It is the same love in nature and quality. As every drop of the sea is the same for quality, so every drop of love which falls on the hearts of believers from Christ's heart is of the self-same nature and is the same quality which the Father bears to him. Indeed, there is a difference in the quantity. And the reason is because our cisterns are not so spacious as Christ's cistern. And yet as much as we can contain, we shall have.

So, in this is the first thing regarding the transcendency of Christ's love to believers: it is the same in nature as that which the Father shows to himself. Christ both did, does, and will declare the Father's name to believers so that the same love by which the Father loved him may be in them, as he himself is in them (John 17).

2. If we consider the degrees in which Christ shares his love with believers, we shall easily see it is transcendent in that also. Christ fills the heart of believers with as much love as they can hold. As the nature of Christ's love is infinitely high, the degree of his love is infinitely full. The prophet Jeremiah, speaking of God's wrath against sinners, uses a metaphor in which he compares God's wrath to wine (as does the psalmist in Psalm 75:8). When explaining the degree of wrath that will be poured out on unforgiven sinners, he says, "Every bottle shall be filled with wine," (Jer. 13:12). Christ's love is also compared to *wine* in the Song of Songs 1:4. And if you compare the hearts of believers to bottles (as you may) then certainly know that every heart is full of the wine of Christ's love. The justice of the Father is not more exact to fill the heart of sinners with his wrath than the grace of the Son is free to fill the

hearts of believers with his love. Therefore, he says, "open your mouth wide, and I will fill it," (Psa. 81:10).

When a box of ointment is opened, the whole house was filled with its odor (John 13:3). Such a box of ointment is the heart of Christ (as may be gathered from Song of Songs 1:3) which, when opened in the houses, *i.e.* the hearts of believers, fills them with its sweet savor. And indeed, Christ bids believers to ask the Father, that their joy might be full. He is as bountiful as his Father, so even without their asking he fills them with his love. In this life believers have as much love as faith can let in. And if the soul is not full, it is only because the mouth is narrow (as the bottle with the narrow neck in the ocean). So, the transcendent fulness of that degree in which Christ shares his love with believers declares the love to be transcendent also.

3. Add to these the duration of Christ's love to believers, and this will further demonstrate its transcendency. As the nature is high, and the degree full, so the duration is *constant* and *perpetual.* Having loved his own, he loved them, "to the end," (John 13:1). In addition to a span of time, this phrase may also indicate that he loves his own to perfection. Christ's love is once and forever. It is of the same nature as Christ himself, making it unchangeable. As nothing in believers was so good as to cause him to love them, nothing is so bad as can cause him to withdraw his love again. Indeed, sometime the visible demonstrations may be concealed, but still the love itself remains sure and is never violated.

As the divines say of Christ on the cross, the beatifical vision was suspended, but the hypostatical union was not dissolved. In like manner, though the light of Christ's love may be obscured for a time, yet the life thereof is still preserved. The love may be dark sometime, but it never dies. There is nothing that can totally or finally separate Christ's love from a believer's soul. Paul asks the question, "what shall separate?" (Rom. 8:35). "The mountains shall depart, and the hills shall be removed," (Christ says), "but my kindness shall not depart," (Isa. 54:10). Believers, when you observe those high hills and mighty mountains which you behold and are amazed at their vastness, keep in mind that those very hills and mountains will one day be gone. But the love of Christ toward you is so transcendently high and sure that it cannot depart. The very heavens themselves wax old like a garment, and yet the person of Christ remains. Even so shall heaven and earth and every creature on earth one day grow old, decay, and die. But the love of Christ toward believers shall forever continue young, fresh, and flourishing. Such is its duration; such shall be its continuance. Indeed, the very life of Christ would have to extinguish; he would have to die again before his love to his own can decay. For his love is not only the believer's life; it is his own life. This transcendent love shall endure forever.

4. Consider finally the operation of Christ's love to believers, and you will see its transcendency equally demonstrated as it was in its nature, degree, and

duration. We guess at the transcendency of things by the nobility of their operations. It is a certain rule, the more noble anything operates, the more noble it is in itself. Of all the affections, love is the most noble, so it follows that love has the most noble operations. Christ's love will easily appear to be transcendent if we consider how much more nobly it operates than any other love in the world. From the first point of time until now, yes, and until time shall be no more, the operations of Christ's love to believers have been, are, and shall be transcendently glorious and noble.

I shall not attempt to search into all actions of Christ, because I shall speak to some of them individually later. However, I will here offer five examples, and in them you shall see the transcendent operations of the love of Christ to believers.

1.) There is no condition so low to which Christ will not condescend to declare his transcendent love. High love stoops low; and the higher the love is, the lower it stoops. If you consider love's elevation by its condescension, you will observe that the lower it condescends, the higher it must elevate. I think it was merely an imaginative story that reported a great prince who took on himself both the form and employment of a laborer to build a house for his beloved in order that he might visit her. Let me tell you, it is not fiction, but a reality in Jesus Christ, that out of the height of his love to believers, he took on himself both the form and the employment of humanity, so that he might declare not only his obedience to his Father, but his love to believers. He emptied himself of royalty and took on the form of a servant, (Phil. 2:7). Christ temporarily laid aside his regal reputation that his love to believers might be of high reputation. O! how nobly did Christ's love operate toward believers, when he stooped so low for their sakes!

2.) There was no action so base which he did not cheerfully undertake to declare his love to believers. Royal love must demean itself to perform the basest service in order that it might declare itself. Jacob chose to be a servant, tending sheep in the heat of summer and the cold of winter, rather than not show his love to Rachel. And this Jesus Christ washed his disciple's feet. Though he is Lord of all, he made himself a servant to all his disciples that he may not only teach them humility and how to love one another, but also that he may declare the height and transcendency of his own love to them all.

3.) There is no failing so sinful which he does not pardon in order to declare the surpassing greatness of his love to believers. Great love pardons great faults; and the greater the faults, the greater the love by which they are pardoned. Peter failed grossly when he denied the Lord, his Master. But Christ's love was transcendent when it forgave Peter. And what failing is more shocking against the bed of love than adultery? Surely the sons of men will not overlook it; this fault transcends their love. And yet, though men will not, Christ does, (Jer. 3:1). His love transcends this fault. Christ's love to believers is far greater than the love of men to their wives, and therefore he does that which they will not, *i.e.* forgive the failing of adultery. The prophet clearly and precisely speaks this of Christ, for he alone is married to believers. It is the glory of man's love to pass by an offence. It is much more the glory of Christ's love that shows itself transcendently glorious in its operation by pardoning the greatest failings of believers.

4.) There was no gift so great which Christ did not bestow on believers. Love *gives.* Isaac's love to Rebecca was great, as evidenced by the great gifts he sent her – a gold earring of half a shekel weight and two gold bracelets of ten shekels weight (Gen. 24:22). Christ gives grace (which is far more precious than gold) to believers. Out of his fulness we receive grace for grace (John 1:16). So great was his bounty, and so large were his gifts that he became poor for our sakes, that by his poverty we might be made rich (2 Cor. 8:9). What greater gift can he give than himself? Such is the transcendent operation of Christ's love, that he gave himself for believer's sakes.

5.) Such is the transcendent love of Christ to believers that there is nothing so base in them that he does not esteem it. Love esteems everything in its beloved. Christ both prizes and praises base things in believers because his love toward them is mighty. Their voice, though inarticulate, is sweet, (Song of Songs 2:10). Their love, though faint, is fair with him, (4:10). Their gifts, though small, are so prized that wherever the gospel of his love is preached, the gifts of their love shall also be divulged, (Mark 14:9). How transcendently glorious and noble the love of Christ operates toward believers! And what does it declare but this, that the love of Christ is indeed transcendent, passing knowledge?

Having briefly touched on some demonstrations of the transcendency of Christ's love to believers, I shall now add a word or two to show the same from some considerable circumstances.

There are four circumstances which I shall mention, namely, the consideration of: 1) the person loving, 2) the persons loved, 3) the time of this love, and 4) the end of that love.

1). Consider the person loving, *i.e.* Jesus Christ who is himself transcendent. It follows, therefore, that his love is also transcendent. *Persona est amoris mensura*, according to the dimension of the person, so are the dimensions of the affection. The height of the lover determines the height of the love. So, we may conclude the greatness of the love from the greatness of him by whom it is declared. A little wrath revealed by God is great because he himself is infinitely great. And a little love shared by Christ must be great love also because he is great. A fire is measured by the quality of combustible material fueling it. Love is fire, and the flames of love transcend and exceed, according to the vastness of the heart in which it burns. Fire in wood makes a great flame and gives a great heat, but fire in brimstone flames more and burns hotter. Christ's love is as fire in brimstone and must needs give a great heat and make a great light. Such light will reveal his love to be transcendent. As the man is, so is his strength (Judges 8:11). As the Lord is, so is his love. He is wonderful, so his love must necessarily be wonderful too. Because we are finite beings, our love cannot be great; and because Christ is infinitely great, his love cannot be little. The love of the Lord Jesus can only be transcendent, passing knowledge, because he himself is such.

2). Now consider the people beloved, and when joined with the former, will clearly demonstrate that the love of Christ is transcendent. Who are the believers, that are in this way beloved? Are they of any note or name? Not at all. Scripture even refers to those whom Christ loves as, "worms," (Isa. 41:14), for we are nothing but poor worms. "For he knows our frame; he remembers that we are dust," (Psa. 103:14). That Christ who is so mighty should love believers so base, that he who is infinitely pure, without spot or blemish, should open his heart to those who are blemished throughout, heightens the love indeed. This demands a transcendent love. He that knows how worthless, contemptible creatures are without Christ will quickly conclude that this quality of love certainly passes knowledge.

3). If we consider the time of love, either when it was first set, or first given forth, we shall see by this also that it is transcendent. For Christ loved believers before the beginning of time. Before the earth came into being, love was present in Christ's heart toward believers. Before the foundation of the world was laid, the foundation of this transcendent love was already in place.

Surely, if Christ delighted in "the sons of men," (Prov. 8:31), *i.e.* believers, before the fountains of the deep were strengthened, or the foundations of the earth were appointed, then certainly his love was also toward them before that time, for his love was the ground of that delight. And if this love began before time, then certainly it is a love that passes knowledge.

The prophet tells us that Christ's love was first declared when we were most unlovely, when no one should pity us. But then Christ passed by and it was the time of his love, and so his love broke forth with the light of life (*cf.* Ezek. 16).

Christ fancied his beloved, all smeared with a poisoned hand and leprous from sin. And yet Christ was as constant in love as ever. The truth and the transcendency of Christ's love to believers is evidenced throughout scriptural history when believers were afflicted with the leprosy of sin and lay dying by the wayside. Each time Jesus Christ came and took them by the hand and opened the love of his heart by pouring forth a stream of blood to wash them and make them clean and whole. Now, before ever the fountains of the deep were laid, a fountain of love sprang up in Christ's heart to believers. What does this declare, but that

Christ's love to believers is transcendent, and passes knowledge!

4). Lastly, consider that end which Christ aims at in his love to believers, and this will declare it also to be transcendent. Christ's love to believers is its own end. He loves that he may love; and this makes the love glorious. All the love which he bestows on you, Christ does not aim at himself, but at you. He loves you now, that he may love you forever. The end which he drives at in declaring love in a lesser measure here is that he may declare love to you in a greater measure hereafter. He makes you vessels of grace in this world, that you may be vessels of glory in that which is to come. All the glory which he aimed at for himself was the glory of his grace, and that shall be toward you. Christ delights to set the golden apple of his glory in the silver picture of your good. He, being love, only aims that men may see the light thereof, and he chose your hearts as the golden candlesticks to set up the glorious light of his love to shine in.

That such an infinite majesty as Christ should love such worms as believers, and that he should set his love toward us before the foundation of the world and shed it abroad in our hearts in the worst of times for our good and his glory as the end, is certainly beyond comprehension. O! Who can consider this without being filled with wonder and crying out, "O! the transcendency of Christ's love!" How it passes our knowledge! Having demonstrated this truth a little, I will now apply this present point in three *uses*.

Namely, 1) of consolation, 2) of conviction, 3) of counsel.

1.) Inasmuch as Christ loves believers with a transcendent love, believers may be comforted at all times! O believing soul, you complain that the world does not love you. You may even say the world *hates* you. Nevertheless, be of good comfort, for Christ loves you; and the world cannot hate you more than he will love you. His love transcends the world's hatred. What the angel told Daniel, I repeat to every grieving soul who lives under the hatred of the world (Dan. 10:19), "Fear not, O man *greatly beloved.*" Why do you complain for want of the puddle drops of the creature's love? You have the pure spring of Christ's love. What weakness is it to cry for want of the light of the stars when you have the light of the sun? You have the Creator's love; do not be sad, therefore, for lacking the love of the creature, especially considering what a transcendent love you have from the Creator. Comfort yourselves with these thoughts: Jesus Christ loves you, and that love of his which he bears to you passes knowledge.

2.) Let this be a word of conviction to sinners. You should be convinced, O sinners, that however you say nobody regards believers, yet there is one who is greater than all who regards them, and that in a high manner. Know that Christ loves them with a transcendent love. You break their souls in pieces, you slay them, and you murder them; and yet you say the Lord does not see, neither does the God of Israel regard it (Psa. 94:7). But be convinced now to the contrary. The Lord Jesus does see, and he does regard them; and before long he will make you know that no matter how you deal with them, they are dear to him. *You* may not love them at all, yet *he* loves them highly. "Were you not afraid," God says, "to speak against my servant Moses?" (Num. 12:8). God is amazed that his enemies were not afraid to speak against a man whom he loved so much. How, then, can any sinner be so vile as to speak and act cruelly against those whom Christ loves transcendently? I pity you if you think that Christ slights them as you do. Rather, be convinced and take heed hereafter what you do. For whoever you oppose, if they are believers, be convinced that the Lord Jesus loves them all with a transcendent love.

3.) This doctrine might be a counselor, as it counsels all to seek out a part in the love of Christ above all the loves of the world. O friends, why do you spend yourselves and lay out your souls in the pursuit of that which is not love, at least not transcendent love? I wish you would now be wise, you who court the creature, court them now no more. I show you a more excellent way of love. Consider the transcendent love of the Lord Jesus and be counseled to labor to get a share in it. O! that hearing this truth that Christ loves believers with a transcendent love might make you sick in your souls, until you participate in this love.

When one heard of the great love which was between two choice friends, he said, *utinam tertius essem, i.e.,* "O! that I were but a third, that I might share with them in their great love." Consider this: you have heard of the high transcendent love which is between Christ and believers; be on fire, therefore, and burn with desire, that you may partake of that love, and that at least you may enjoy that love which those who have are unable to express, or conceive, as it is a transcendent love, a love that *passes knowledge.*

Sermon 3

"And to know the love of Christ, which passes knowledge, that you might be filled with all the fulness of God," (Eph. 3:19).

We are launched out into the great depth of our Savior's love in which our souls may contentedly swim as we consider this doctrine. And although I can neither sound ground nor see shore, I desire to remain in this sea; for it would be a delight of the highest manner to be drowned here. The love of Christ is so surpassingly sweet, and so infinitely necessary for our souls, that I desire to make further discovery of its transcendency.

The apostle uses hyperbole to express the greatness of Christ's love by describing it as a love that passes knowledge. We have already explained the meaning of the expression and began the proof of this point of doctrine, that Christ's love for believers is a *transcendent* love. As this is the main thing which I see in the text, and indeed the main thing which every soul ought to see and build their life on, I shall proceed to speak of this further here.

The last time I demonstrated this truth in a general way. I shall, therefore, now go on to demonstrate the love of Christ to be transcendent from a brief survey of the course of his life.

Indeed, Christ's life was one great act of love, begun at his birth and carried on even to the time of his death and ascension. If we follow this Lamb in the whole course of his life, we shall see that from the cradle to the cross, to his return to the Father, the entire path was paved with love.

I shall now touch on three demonstrations which show the transcendency of Christ's love to believers in its glorious fullness. They are: 1.) his birth and incarnation, 2.) his life and conversation, and, 3.) his death and passion. Each of these seriously considered will abundantly demonstrate that the love of Christ to believers is transcendent.

First, consider his birth and incarnation. How does Christ's love transcend in this act? The low condescension of Christ, in becoming man, overwhelmingly declares the high transcendency of his love to believers. Had it not been for the great love in the Lord Jesus, he could have taken on an angelic nature instead. If Christ had come into the world with tidings of love and life, he might have come as an angel of glory instead of a piece of clay. But he passed by the nature of angels and took on himself the nature of man, that in this act he may declare love to believers. The apostle tells us in Hebrews 2:16, "For *verily* he took not on him the nature of angels...," *i.e.* in no way and by no means would he take on the angelical nature. But rather he took on himself the seed of Abraham in order that he might declare his love to the children of Abraham. That we may see a little more clearly how the love of Christ transcends in his birth, I shall speak to this point in some particulars; and by all of them you shall see how Christ's love shines gloriously in this act of his, when he became man and was born for their sakes.

Here I will consider particularly these four things regarding his incarnation which evidence the transcendency of Christ's love: 1.) where Christ came from, 2.) where Christ came to, 3.) how Christ came, and 4.) why Christ came.

1.) Where he came from. Christ was in the heart of the Father, where he lived in his Father's love. He came from the presence of his Father to earth to declare God's love to believers. John tells us he came down from heaven (John 6:38). Jesus Christ from all eternity was in heaven. There he had his Father's company; there he enjoyed his Father's love. There he was blessed in his Father's heart (John 1:18). He was living in the light of the Father's love. And being with God, he solaced himself in God. He occupied that very light and glory in which God himself lives. And yet he left all this behind for believers' sakes. He left his Father's house to undertake this long journey. How long a journey did Christ undertake? And what paradise of pleasure did he leave to come to believers when he was born? Surely his affection was great and his love was transcendent to leave for a time the Father's house of love, his Father's heart, to open to believers the fountain of love that was in his own heart for them.

2.) But where did Christ come to, when he came from heaven? Was it into some place of comfort and plenty, some land of light? Was it into some paradise, some land of life? Was it into some place of pleasure? Not at all. The place he came was Egypt, where believers sat in darkness. It was the wilderness, where believers lived under the shadow of death. It was into this world, where everything is vanity and vexation. Christ came here for believers' sakes. And what transcendent love brought Christ here? He saw that his beloved ones were in a defiled place, a place which could not be their rest (Micah 2:10). His love therefore prevailed with him to come here, to fetch his beloved to himself. It was great love which Abimelech the Ethiopian showed to Jeremiah when he came to the brink of that filthy dungeon in which the prophet was and put down cords to draw him out. But what great love would it have been if, instead of coming to the brink of the dungeon, Abimelech had come down into the dungeon and not only drew him up with ropes, but carried him up in his arms? This would have been love indeed.

Let me tell you, believers, that you were in a worse dungeon than Jeremiah, dying for hunger and drowning in the mire. And when the Lord Jesus Christ came, it was not only to the brink of the dungeon with cords to draw you up, but into the dungeon itself, to take you up into his very heart, and to rescue you from perishing. "I came forth from the Father," says Christ, which was great love. But he adds, "I came into the world," (John 16:28). Here was love indeed, that Christ came from the Father's throne into the world, Satan's kingdom. Christ came from the place in which glory shines (heaven) unto a place where evil thrives (the world). Christ left the presence of the Father who always smiled upon him, to come to the place of men who frowned upon him. For him to come from heaven where he always heard the *hallelujahs* of angels, to come to earth where his ears were filled with the insults of sinners shows the measure of his love. O! the height and the depth! O! the breadth and length! O! the transcendency of Christ's love to believers!

3.) But how did Christ come here? Did he come in pomp with glory? Did he come with the sound of a trumpet, that all might know that he was a prince? No, he came to earth in a lowly, humble manner. When Christ was born, indeed a heavenly host appeared, praising God and singing. But that was to announce to the world that the Messiah had come more than it was to dignify his coming. As Isaiah 42:2 states, "He shall not cry, nor lift up, nor cause his voice to be heard in the street." In other words, Christ did not come in an outward glorious fashion with pomp, but in a silent way. He came to do all that for his own, according to the Father's predetermined plan. And if you consider the history of his nativity, you will say that Christ did not come with any great show; he was born, not as the son of some great queen, but the infant of a poor virgin. His reputed father was not a mighty monarch, but a mean carpenter. "Is not this the carpenter's son?" He was born, not in a mansion, but in a manger. His traveling mother lay in the manger with him and there he was born. Wrapped in some homely cloths, his mother laid him in the cradle. He that sat upon the throne amidst the cherubim was content to be born in such a place. In this way, we must conclude that Christ's love was surpassingly great in that he would agree to be so little, in a human way, and to lie so low for your sakes.

4.) Join to all these the end of Christ's coming into the world, and this will exceedingly heighten the demonstration that the love of Christ passes knowledge. Why, for what did he come? Why did the king of glory come from heaven to earth in such a lowly manner? Did he come to dethrone the kings of the earth and set himself up as Lord of all? Indeed, Herod feared this, but without ground, for Christ came for no such end. The end for which he came was love. His design was to declare and make known that love of God which had been hidden from eternity to believers. Therefore, it was that he was born in time, namely, that believers might see and know that love which he had kept for them from before time existed.

I will in a word mention six particular ends (while omitting others) for which Christ came into the world, and you will see them meet in love at their center.

1.) The first end for which he was born was to redeem the precious souls of believers from the slavery of sin and their bodies from that vanity to which they were subjected. Christ saw his beloved, captives in Satan's kingdom, bound with chains and made slaves to his will. This sight went to his soul, and his love could not contain itself. He had to come that his beloved might be set free. That this was the end of his nativity, as the apostle witnesses in Galatians 4:4, "When the fulness of time was come, God sent his son," (and he readily came), "made of a woman, made under the law, to redeem them that were under the law, that we might receive the adoption of sons." You were once slaves, but Christ was born that you might be sons. A part of that adoption to which you were redeemed is not only the redemption of your souls (though that is the chief part) but also the redemption of your bodies, as is made clear in Romans 8:23. This is why Christ was born, and I think I do not need to say that it was an end of love, for you cannot consider this without confessing that.

2.) Another end which Christ aimed at in his nativity was to be fitted to suffer for believer's sakes. As Christ was God and shined with the glory and majesty of the deity, those who would seize him and accuse him before God's timing allowed could not. John 18:6 states, "As soon then as he had said unto them, 'I am he,' they went backward, and fell to the ground." As God, Christ could not suffer, and yet it was necessary that he suffer the wrath of God for sin for believers' sakes. Therefore, he was contented to cloud the glory of his deity with the mantle of the seed of Abraham, that he might be fitted to suffer for them.

Codrus (a semi-mythical king of Athens) saw that his death would profit his country, and yet he knew that while he had on his imperial robes none could slay him. So, he laid aside the royal robe, and put on the clothing of the poor and homely, that he might be fit to die in that disguise. My beloved, the Lord Jesus saw that the blood of bulls and goats could not take away sins. He also knew that if believers would be spared the wrath of God against sin that it must be by blood. So, the Father prepared him a body (Heb. 10:5). And because his heart had this law of love written in it, he willingly took that body on himself, that in doing so he might be fit to bleed. Surely you are blind if you do not see love in this end, namely, that Christ was born to be fit to die.

3.) A third end for which he was born was that he might be like believers. Love tends to likeness. Because he loved us, Christ was born the God-man that he might be like them in all things, whom he loved above all things. Philippians 2:7 says, "He was made in the likeness of man." He beheld his beloved in the form of servants, and he was born the baby of a virgin that he might be in their form. Christ saw his dear ones, clothed with the sackcloth of human nature, and therefore stooped to a nativity that he might be in the same fashion and appear in the same suit. Though human nature with all its infirmities is a base, plain clothing, yet his divine love made him value it above the form of angels. Therefore, passing by the nature of angels, he took upon him the nature of man and was born that he might be like believers. This is transcendent love.

4.) Christ in his nativity aimed at another end, and that was to unite himself clearly and convincingly with believers. Union is an effect of affection, and love desires to unite. And if union is designed as the end of any act, we may safely say that love was the active agent in that design. Christ indeed unites himself to believers by communicating to them his own divine nature; but that he might make the union more firm, he was born to take upon him their human nature. Believers, Christ is nearer united to you than to the angels. His love for you in this respect transcends his love for them. He did not take upon himself their nature, and so he was not united to them in that way. Rather, he took upon him your nature and was for this end born, that he might be united to you. Is not this transcendent love?

5.) Christ had yet another end of love, for which he was born, namely that he might be fitted in a more familiar manner to condescend to humanity's limited capacities and sympathize with the infirmities of believers. Christ desires to converse with them sweetly and to sympathize with them seriously; clearly neither of which he could do as God. Therefore, God foreordained that he would be born as a *man*. As he was God, and had only the divine nature, believers were not able to converse with him. His glory was so amazing that their weak eyes could not behold it. His majesty was so overpowering that frail spirits could not converse with it. He was therefore pleased to take our nature that we might participate in his grace and be saved. Otherwise, who could behold fully his glory and live? Had Jesus Christ took upon him the nature of angels and come into the world as such, his presence would have been frightening. Believers could not have borne it. For this end, therefore, "the word was made flesh and dwelt amongst us," (John 1:14), so that we might behold the glory of God in the only begotten son. The divine glory could be more safely contemplated by believers while it was in the tent of flesh than it could be in its pure form.

Now believers may look upon the luster of his deity more sweetly, while they can behold it through the brotherhood of humanity. It behooved him in all things to be made like unto his brethren, that he might show tender mercy or pity on us (Heb. 2:17). By being born a man who experienced the infirmities of human nature, Christ can now sympathize with the sufferings of his children. He could have solaced himself in the contemplation of his own glory, never stooping to the pain of our infirmities. Yet he was born to humanity that we might behold his glory, and that he might sympathize with us. He condescended to our infirmities and participated in our humanity in his birth. Is this not an infinitely transcendent love?

6.) Finally, by his nativity Christ elevates our humanity to the level of dignity that we had before the fall, having been made in the image of God. Humanity was imputed into the nature of God at the birth of his Son, and by uniting your nature to his own, he imputes his righteousness into your humanity, restoring its dignity! How does the human nature shine in the luster of the divine? How does the nature of man glister in the golden, glorious ring of the divine nature? Through the transcendency of Christ's love, because he stooped so low. He was born for this end, to raise high the nature of his beloved ones!

You can now see how the birth of Christ, when thoroughly considered, brings a fresh discovery of the transcendency of his love. Certainly, if you spiritually contemplate all that love which shines in the birth of the Lord Jesus, you will easily conclude that his love to believers passes knowledge.

The second position from which I will demonstrate the transcendency of Christ's love is the life of Christ. You must not think that I dare undertake the whole history of his life in order to demonstrate his transcendent love from every act, for this would be too large a field to walk in. I shall speak generally of it, and then I shall discuss in a more particular manner some remarkable passages that relate more specifically to his transcendent love to believers.

Generally, the life of Christ was a perfect mirror of his love. Every aspect of his life exuded his love, and if we put all the actions of his life together, we may conclude that he was born not so much to live as to love. There was not a word which dropped from his lips, but it was full of love. And for his works which he did, they all spoke love so loudly that the deafest ear might hear it. In fact, we may say (as the psalmist does in another case) that there is no speech, nor language, where the voice of his love was not heard. This thread runs through every act of his life. If we begin at the temple, where he disputed with the doctors, and follow him to the mount, where he was crucified by the soldiers, we see the entire path covered with love-roses. And as there is no beam in the sun in which there is no light, so there was no act in the life of Christ that does not shine with the light of love. But here I shall instance five particulars and show how Christ in the actions of his life declared the transcendency of his love.

1.) Jesus Christ, for believer's sakes, experienced all the human miseries of this life. You cannot experience any human misery that Christ does not understand as part of his humanity. This truth sweetens your suffering if you will allow it. Are you hungry? So was he (Matt. 4:3). Are you thirsty? So was he. Are you weary? He was too (John 4:6). Do you meet with derisions and persecutions? The Lord Christ out of his transcendent love experienced all these in his life for you. Believers, I urge you to remember that when you meet with any of the miseries of this life, your beloved has already met with them for your sakes that he might sweeten them to your souls. And therefore, when you are pressed by the miseries of this life in any kind, think upon your Savior's love who lived a life exposed to all these same miseries because of his love for you. And I have no doubt that you will say, O transcendent love!

2.) The Lord Jesus submitted to all the duties of religion not only to fulfill the righteousness of the law but to declare the infiniteness of his love. For by it believers may see that at no time does he require more of them than he did himself. This is why the yoke of Christ is "easy," (Matt. 11:30). His commandments do not appear grievous because he obeyed them first himself. There is no duty to which you can be called in the whole course of your life but that your Savior in his life has fulfilled. The child may well say he has a loving father when he can see him first doing whatever he commands the child to do. Your everlasting God, Jesus Christ, performed in his life all those duties you are to do in religion. Is this not transcendent love?

3. Our Lord, on the whole course of his life, was ever careful to provide and use all possible means for the strengthening of believers' graces. Knowledge and faith are the two great graces for the sweetening of the life of believers, and Christ was very careful to strengthen them. Therefore, he chiefly spoke to those things which would strengthen these graces. For knowledge, how lovingly did he speak about that which his disciples were able to bear? And if he thought they did not understand what he said, how lovingly did he expound all things to them when they were alone? (Mark 4:33-34). When they asked him about the meaning of any parable, how lovingly he responded, telling them that it was their privilege as his children to know the mysteries of the kingdom of God (Luke 8:9-10). And even when

they did not ask, Jesus knew when they were confused about his teachings. And in those times, he voluntarily (without being asked) explained what they needed to hear to be clear of his meaning (Matt. 16:7-9).

As for faith, it is easy to observe how ready Christ was to strengthen it. Did he not rejoice when he had an opportunity so to do? Make a note of that in Job 11. And when Lazarus was dead, he knew how his raising of him would confirm their faith, which is why he said that he was glad, for their sakes, that he was not there when Lazarus died, so they may believe (verse 15). What does this care of Christ to strengthen your graces declare, but the transcendency of his love to your souls?

4.) In his earthly ministry, Jesus Christ was concerned more for, and rejoiced more in believers' comforts than his own. When he heard that great voice from heaven, saying, "I have glorified it," (*i.e.* his name) "and I will glorify it," he said that this voice came not for his sake but for his disciples. It seems his end in that request (for that voice was an answer to his prayer) was not his glory but their good. And therefore, not rejoicing himself in the excellent glory of that voice from heaven, he speaks to them, and applies it to them, professing it was for their sakes (John 12:30). In the same way, when he was to die, and knew that his hour was come, he was more focused on comforting his disciples, that in so doing he might declare that, "having loved them, he loved them to the end," with a transcendent love, (John 13:1). Tell me, my beloved, should you see one going to the stake or scaffold to die, and you observe him spending all his time, breath, and energy in comforting someone he dearly loves, would you not say that his love transcended in making him forget himself to comfort her? So, it was with your Savior. With only a few hours left before he was to be arrested and beaten, he was concerned for the comfort of his disciples more than his own. He spends all this time laboring to silence their despair and sorrows, disregarding his own pending sufferings and death. What transcendent love!

Lastly, it must be also considered that with the last action in his earthly life he declared the transcendency of his love by putting up more requests on behalf of believers than for himself. You know the prayer in John 17. And if you observe it, you shall find that although in the beginning he prays for himself, "Father the hour is come, glorify thy son," yet apart from reiterating this request in verse 5, he shuts himself out of all the rest of the prayer and spends it wholly for believers. And what glorious things he requested on their behalf, that the Father would keep and preserve them (ver. 15), that he would own and sanctify them (ver. 10, 17), that they might be one with the Father, as he was one (ver. 21-22), and in closing, he intreats the Father to admit them to be there where he was, in order that they may behold his glory! And how strongly does he argue for this? Does he not use the cogent motive of love? "For you love me," (verse 24). It is as if he should say, "Father, I know you love me, you did so before ever the world was. Now I beseech you, by that same love to own, preserve, sanctify, and make one with thyself these you have given me, as I am yours. And let them whom I loved in the world be with me when they leave the world. O Father, as you love me, hear and grant this request for my beloved ones." Tell me now, how transcendent is Christ's love? And how near are believers to his heart? Our Savior, as the hour of his death draws near, forgets himself and breathes out his last requests on behalf of his beloved.

Do you see how easy it is to look at the separate incidents throughout the life of Christ and to note in every single one his transcendent love to believers? But I must now speak a word to the death of Christ, and you shall see this also as a lively demonstration of the truth that the love of Christ to believers passes knowledge.

As the third leg of demonstrations is that of the death of Christ, I shall speak to it a little more distinctly, though briefly. But where shall we begin his passion? And at what part of it shall we enter into this demonstration? Shall we go with him into the garden where it began, or shall we ascend Mount Calvary where it ended, or shall we speak of what he suffered in the high priest's hall?

How transcendently sweet is our Savior's love beginning in the garden where he was arrested. Believers see him there, when his soul began to be sorrowful and very heavy, and listen to what he said, "my soul is exceeding sorrowful, even unto death," (Matt. 26:38).

Tell me, saints, what manner of love is this? Your Lord is *sad unto death* in order that he might remove those clouds which sometimes keep your souls in the shadows of death and darkness. But go on and listen to your Lord's cry to the Father, once and again, when he begged that the cup might pass from him. Surely the wrath in the bottom of the cup was very bitter, as he desired to be delivered from it. But as surely the love in Christ's bosom was very sweet, which prevailed with him to submit his will to the Father's and to drink it up for your sake. Did you ever hear of sweating in a cold night on the cold ground in an open garden? Surely, he must have been hot within, or else he could not have done so. Indeed, the heat of your Savior's love was such that it allowed him to bear the heat of God's wrath, so much so that he sweated clots of blood (his veins leaked his lifeblood under the pressure and tension he experienced while the cold air congealed it). And this was only the beginnings of his suffering. For your sakes, believers, you would be blind if you cannot see his matchless love in this. Some have written letters to their beloved with their blood. What a sweet truth, however, that Christ in the garden bled enough to write a large letter of love to you. And yet if you read such love rightly, you cannot express the extent of his agony in the garden. The greatness of Adam's sin in eating the forbidden fruit in the Garden of Eden was not as powerful as the transcendency of Christ's love in his agony in the Garden of Gethsemane.

For his love is what reinstates believers into a happier state than the Eden paradise was or ever could be.

Let us follow our Lord now from the garden to the high priest's hall, where he encounters the hideous outcries and rude rabble against him. Was it not love that stopped our Savior's ears and silenced his tongue, that he would not reply? You read how some spat on him and others railed at him, how some blasphemed him, and others bullied him; how many scoffed, how many scorned, how many accused, how all cried out against him. And when you read all this, do you not sense the sweet, transcendent love of Christ to you?

Let us now follow Christ to Calvary. See him nailed to the cross for your sakes, and tell me, does this sight not confirm this truth, namely that the love of Christ passes knowledge? Surely, believers, Christ's hanging on the cross, then breathing out his last breath, and pouring out his heart's blood in a shameful, cursed, and tormenting way for your sakes is enough to make you cry out, "O the depth of his love!" It was well said by one that Mount Calvary was love's academy. And he that cannot learn the transcendency of Christ's love to believers here is worse than a dunce.

The blood of the cross speaks love in strength, and no other such sermon of love in the Bible, nor in creation, demonstrates it so. "Greater love than this hath no man that a man lay down his life for his friends," (John 15:13). Indeed, man is not capable of a greater love than Jesus Christ had and showed, for he laid down his life for his foes (which believers were). It was but a brag of Peter's when he said he would die for Christ. But it was a *reality* in Christ's words.

Certainly, it was his transcendent love that strengthened his soul until he tasted death for you. The Scriptures record the character of the martyr's love for Christ when they willingly died for his sake.

But their death for Christ was their duty (they were bound to it because Christ loved them), whereas Christ's love to us is grace, for he loved us first. It is as if the prince's son goes to his Father, the king, and says, "Father, I confess that this condemned malefactor deserves to die, but I see a willingness in you that he should live. Nevertheless, it contradicts your justice. You magnify your mercy in his pardon, could you also satisfy your justice? For that, Father, here I am, and I give myself up to die to satisfy your justice, only let this poor wretch live to the glory of your person and my free grace. I will go to the place of execution and die in his stead." Ask the malefactor what kind of love he counts this to be. Believers, ask your own hearts (for you were the malefactors) and tell me, what word is great enough to define the great love of Christ, which he lively expressed in his death for you? Surely you will say, the measure of his love is too large; you cannot through your limited capacities express such a love adequately.

I must profess it, and can you? Truly, I cannot. This topic is more fitted to meditation than expression. And yet if we meditate on it for the whole of life, we can never reach the height of it. The thoughts of Christ's life are swallowed up by the thoughts of his death. I will wind up this point with this conclusion. You are not scholars in Christ's school if you cannot read a large and long lecture of love about the cross of Christ. For the love of Christ expressed in his death transcends so high above our thoughts that we shall never be able to come to the height of it for all our life. His love transcends our expressions and confounds our conceptions, and yet it must be believed and applied.

At present, I shall offer but three words to help you in the application of the transcendency of Christ's love to believers.

1.) First, stand and wonder, believing souls, at this love. Indeed, it is fitted much more for wonder than words. Think about what I have said and let your thoughts dwell upon its meditations. And when, after doing so you have reached some heightened understanding, then in the wonderment of your souls cry out, "O the depth of the love of Christ, which passes knowledge!" Wonder and say, "Lord Jesus, what is man, and what am I, that you should be mindful of me? How is it that you were born for me? You lived and died to declare your love to me!" O that you would lose yourselves in the thoughts of your Savior's love! And when you have lost yourselves in the bottomless gulf of your Lord's love, then recover your spirits again, and cry out, "O the dazzling heights! O the confounding (yet comfortable) depths! O the divine (yet immensurable) dimensions of the love of Christ, which passes knowledge!"

2.) Lament! O believers, lament when you consider that regardless of how much Christ loves you, you are too apt to neglect his love. One holy man wept when he saw his heart so dull that he could not consider the love of Christ as he should and would. And truly, who can consider with a dry eye the neglect of our thoughts of the transcendent love of Christ? Does Christ love you so much, and yet you think of him so little? Can you spend days and weeks reading fictional stories of love and yet not have an hour to meditate on the real, regal love of the Lord Jesus? What small returns of love does Christ receive from you in return? He loves us richly; but, alas, we love him poorly. His love passes knowledge; none can understand it. But our love, in a sad sense, passes knowledge too, for none can perceive it. How little do we forsake for Christ, when he forsook all for us?

He forsook heaven and came into the world for us; and we will not forsake earth for him. He did much for us and counted it but little. He lived the whole of his life for us; but we do so little for him, and yet we count it much, grudging to give him the last and least, though Satan gets the first and most part of our life. He suffered for us even death itself; but which of us is willing to taste suffering for him? True, some have said if they had a thousand heads, they would lose them all for Christ, but whom among us would lose our one head for him?

Ignatius of old said he was willing to endure fire, cross, butcheries, and all for Christ. But in these latter days, though Christ's love is hot, ours has grown cold; we can scarcely endure a word, a jeer, a scoff for Christ. Well, I urge you to sit, and sigh, and say, "O! How we ignore the love of Christ!" He was born, he lived, and he died out of love for us. But we are so far from dying for Christ that we scarcely are willing to live for him.

3.) Thirdly, in as much as Christ loves you with a transcendent love, be content even if you do not have the love of men. It is a shame that any who are the beloved of Christ should mourn for not being loved by man. Why should the king's daughter weep because the servants scorn her, because the king himself embraces her? You should rest, satisfied and content, in Christ's love that is so transcendent. Drink waters out of your own cistern! Christian, rejoice with the Lord who loves you! Let him be as, "the loving hind and pleasant roe; let his breasts satisfy thee at all times," (Prov. 5:19). Do not mourn for the loss of creature love, but rather be ravished always with his love. Bathe yourself in Christ's heart and be content with his love. Be reminded that the love of Christ for you passes knowledge, and you cannot be discontented at the lack of love from any or all the creatures. It is a sign that the love of Christ passes knowledge and that its value is transcendent, for in the absence of all other loves, you cannot help but be content and satisfied with this.

Sermon 4

"And to know the love of Christ, which passes knowledge, that ye might be filled with all the fulness of God," (Eph. 3:19).

We are currently looking at the transcendency of Christ's love to believers, and O! how sweet it is to lose ourselves in this consideration! How hard it is to leave a point of such infinite necessity and sweetness. How gladly could I not only live, but also die while declaring the love of Christ to believers! At the very mention that his love to believers is a transcendent love makes our hearts leap for joy. Tell me, O believer, could you not wish to have your mind and heart continually attuned to the truth that Christ loves you with a love that passes knowledge? Something we have already hinted at, and something more we shall add at this time, is that when I have said all that I can about the transcendency of Christ's love to believers, I shall come many thousand steps short of its height. For that reason, I am resolved to say all that I intend to say on this point at this time.

Therefore, with a little more to demonstrate that the love of Christ passes knowledge, I shall encourage you to see 1.) his command over them, 2.) his care for them, and, 3) his endeavor to not only declare but to persuade believers of this love.

1.) First, if we consider the command which Christ exercises over believers, we shall see the transcendency of his affection even in that. It is Christ's glory that he is the King of the saints (in a peculiar manner) and through his grace he exercises that kingly power in a sweet way. He rules the nation with a rod of iron, yet he rules the saints with a golden scepter. So although in wrath, his iron rod breaks the nations in pieces, his golden scepter is still stretched out in love to entertain the saints. You read in Song of Songs 3 that Solomon made a chariot of the wood of Lebanon, he made the pillars of silver, the bottom of gold, the covering of purple, and inlaid the anterior with love (Song of Songs 3:10). That chariot which Solomon made for himself, and in which he rode, might well describe the chariot in which Christ rides up and down the world of believers whom he governs. Indeed, it is very glorious and glitters with beams of light. But mostly it is very gracious, being paved with stones of love.

Love is the throne on which he sits, love is the scepter with which he rules, and all his government is managed in such a way that believers may say that he is the Lord of love even in his ruling of them. Absalom only flattered the people when he stood by the way of the gate and kissed all that passed by, insinuating how sweetly he would govern if he rose to the kingdom. But that which was flattery in Absalom is reality in Christ. When any of the spiritual pilgrims come (as believers do) to give him respect, he puts forth his hands and takes them and kisses them, and does not only promise, but performs transcendent love in all his commands over them. But to read this more particularly, you will see the transcendency of Christ's love discovered in his command over believers if you consider three things.

First, Christ lays no commands upon believers, but such as are full of love and sweetness. He reduces all the decalogue to these two commands, "Thou shalt love the Lord your God with all your heart, and with all your soul, and with all your mind. And you shalt love your neighbor as yourself," (Matt. 22:37-39). Well might John have said that his commandments are not grievous (1 John 5:3), because the word here is "burdensome," and what burden is there in the commands of Christ unless *love* is a burden? Indeed, it is his prerogative to command what he pleases, but he commanded nothing but what is pleasant in itself and will be so to a sanctified soul. In this we see the transcendency of his love. "A new commandment I give unto you, that ye love one another, as I have loved you, that ye also love one another," (John 13:34). Well may the commandment be called "new," seeing as it was never given by any king besides himself. And surely there was great love in his heart to believers when he only laid a burden, or a command of love upon their shoulders. "All her ways are ways of pleasantness," (Prov. 3:17). The ways of Christ (*i.e.,* his commands) are ways of pleasantness. Believers, if you could but live in love, you would fulfill the law of your Lord. For as a Lord of love to you, love is the fulfilling of the law he lays upon you.

Such is the transcendency of his love to believers, that he commands nothing from them that he did not do himself. Man may think it is a hard and a harsh command to wash the feet of a poor believer, a fellow servant. But grace will see the command to be sweet and lovely. And in love, Christ himself has done it before he commands us to do it. Ask the servant whether his Lord is loving, who lays no commandment upon him but that which is sweet in itself, and sweet in its fruit, and no worse than his Lord himself will undertake. Believers, all the commands of your Lord Christ are sweet in themselves, and sweet in their fruit; and they are such as he himself (while he lived on earth) stooped to do. Does this not declare transcendent love?

Secondly, Christ gives all his commands in love. Whatever he bids believers to do, he does so in a loving way. As the command, so is the manner of its imposing, *i.e.,* sweet and loving. It is possible that a sweet thing may be enjoyed in a harsh way. An easy commandment may be burdensome in the way it is imposed. To command with a bended fist and a frowning forehead is not to command in a loving way. But now Jesus Christ, whenever he commands, he commands sweetly. He does not raise his voice. He does not speak in an austere, rough, rugged manner. But as the Lord is loving, so is his language. Observe how he says, "you are my friends, if you do whatsoever I command you," (John 15:14). He does not threaten and say, "I will be your foe, if you will not obey; but if you do, you shall be my friends." And so again, if you love me, keep my commandments. It is worth noting that grace may be said to come in this respect by Christ. He did not give his law as God did with Moses, with thunder and lightning and in a dreadful manner, but he gave the law to his disciples himself, in a sweet and loving way. He begins his sermons with "blessed are you." And all his commands drop from him like the drops of dew upon the tender grass; "he shall come down like rain upon the mown grass, as showers that water the earth," (Psa. 72:6), *i.e.,* he shall come down both softly and sweetly. Here you may see the transcendency of Christ's love to you, in the way he lays his commandments on you.

Thirdly, consider the end of all Christ's commandments, and here you will also discover the transcendency of his love to believers. He seeks not himself, but them, in all his commands. He bids the believer to work, not that he may reap anything himself, but that the believer may get all. He puts them to work in his vineyard that they may have all the harvest. As it is inconsistent with his deity to have anything added to him, so also it is inconsistent with his love. He has his servants reap that they may have all the corn, and he puts them to work that he may give them wages. "Take my yoke upon you, and you shall find rest for your souls." Christ lays a yoke upon their necks, not to burden them but to ease them; not to break their backs, but to refresh their hearts. In terms of commands, many kings and rulers seek to serve themselves and their own greatness rather than do their subjects good. But Jesus Christ your king is not such a one as this; all that he aims at in his government is for your good. The end of his commandments is your comfort. As his government increases over you, so his peace increases in you. This is the effect and fruit of all his commandments, not so much that others may take notice of his glory in commanding as that you may find his grace in obeying. Indeed, love is the work and wages of his commandments; he bids you do so, that he may love you. Therefore, though you are frail and weak and cannot obey, he will be kind to love you.

Now that we see the commands of Christ are rich with love in their substance, love in their requirements, and love in their aim, what can you conclude but that the love of Christ to believers is transcendent in the exercise of his command over them?

Secondly, consider the care that Christ has of his own. O! the transcendent love that Christ expresses to believers in how he cares for them in all their necessities! He is not only a Lord who commands but a Father who cares and provides for his own. And it is easy to observe transcendency of love in the transcendent care that Christ provides. Food, clothing, and lodging are the least of his provisions; and yet you see Christ not only provides these, but he also gives us many other things.

First, Christ sees that believers have food to eat. He knows they must have bread, and therefore he has provided the bread of life. He knows they must have drink, and therefore he has opened the sealed fountain of the water of life. The care that God took to feed his people in the wilderness demonstrated his love to them. He sent them quail and manna. And when you find yourself in the wilderness of this world, your Lord declares his love by making rich provisions of spiritual food for you. He prepares the hidden manna which he gives you, a feast of fat things, full of marrow, and wine well refined. No, even in the midst of your enemies he has prepared a table for you. And he has made himself meat for you, not only that you may be sure of food, but to ensure that the food might be surpassingly sweet. If it is true that the pelican feeds her young ones with her own blood, then that bird may be a type of your beloved. His flesh is meat indeed, and his blood is drink indeed; and this he gives for the life of your souls.

History tells the story that to vie for Mark Antony's love, Cleopatra dissolved a precious pearl in his drink. Christ has done much more for you, for of what value are corruptible goods such as gold, and silver, and pearls when compared to his precious blood? This is the blood Christ gave believers to drink that they might live forever.

Secondly, Christ has provided not only food for the belly, but raiment for the back too. And as the food, so also the raiment transcends in love. Christ has provided a garment of rich and costly attire for believers. Before Christ, you were spiritually naked and had nothing but the filthy rags of your own works. Then, even then, he clothed you with embroidered work, and shod you with badger's skins, and covered you with fine linen, and decked you with ornaments, and put bracelets on your hands, and a chain on your neck, and a jewel on your forehead and earrings on your ears, and a beautiful crown upon your head. Thus, he adorned you, and thus he arrayed you, and you were exceeding glorious with these righteous garments. The transcendent love of Christ gives to believers the same righteous garments that he himself wears. On the mount of transfiguration, (Matt. 17:2) it is said that his raiment was as white as the light. And when the saints appeared to John in his vision, they appeared in garments of the same color; they were arrayed in white robes (Rev. 7:13). Righteousness is his garment, and so it is believer's too. It was an act of great love to Mordechai that the royal apparel which the king wore was brought and put on him. Such is the transcendent love of Christ to his own that he has the royal apparel which he himself wears brought to you and put on your souls now. And it shall be put on your bodies hereafter; even that body which is now vile shall be made glorious like to his glorious body. And when Christ shall come and appear in his garments of glory, you shall appear with him, and be like him. And then he shall be admired, not only in himself, but in you. O! transcendent love, that Jesus Christ should provide such clothing for us poor creatures!

Thirdly, as for lodging, Christ has provided this for believers as well. Indeed, he himself had no home here on earth (not so much as a hole in which to lay his head). So believers can fare no worse, as we have better lodging here on earth than our Lord had. But as to hereafter, he has provided a mansion for his bride, the church. This mansion is a building of God, a house not made with hands (Heb. 9:11). The Shunammite declared her love to the man of God by making him a little chamber, setting a bed in it, and a table, a stool, and a candlestick for him, (2 Kings 4:10).

Jesus Christ showed greater love than this, however, in providing a better room for believers. He provides not a little chamber but a great mansion. He offers not a stool but a throne, not a candlestick but himself as a light, "Father, I will that they also, whom you hast given me, be with me where I am; that they may behold my glory, which you hast given me: for you loved me before the foundation of the world," (John 17:24). Consider this, believers, that Christ has prepared as good a house for you as for himself and, along with the Father, desires that you should come into his house and dwell with him there.

So that now here is rich provision of necessities, food, clothing, and lodging. And what does this declare but rich love in Christ, that he should take such care of believers in this way?

We might add that not only has Christ prepared these necessities, but he has also prepared other things which are glorious. But who shall be able to declare all the gracious provision which Christ has made for his!

Eye has not seen, neither has ear heard, nor has it entered into the heart of man to conceive those things! We will therefore break out with the psalmist, "O how great is your goodness, which you have laid up as a secret treasure for them that love you, and believe in you," (Psa. 31:19). In this way, you see the transcendent love of Christ in his care for, as well as his command over believers.

Thirdly, we might abundantly demonstrate the transcendency of Christ's love to believers in his endeavor to declare and persuade the hearts of believers of all this love. That Christ should love at all, and love so much is transcendent; but that he should take pains to persuade the hearts of sinners to believe is an added layer to the transcendency of his love. Christ saw how unlikely we would be to believe, and how hardly we would be brought to persuade ourselves that indeed he loved us at all. So he took such great care, and made such provision for the persuading of the hearts of believers to close with the truth that he loved them. "I have declared your name, and will declare it, that the love wherewith you hast loved me may be in them," (John 17:26). This is the great work which he did when he was on earth, and which his ambassadors now do in his name, namely, to persuade the hearts of his own that he loves them. What a great deal of love was there in that cry of his when he was on earth, that if any would come to him, he would in no wise cast them out? And if they were thirsty, they could come to him and drink! How he declared the strength of his love in persuading souls to come to him that they might taste and see how he loved them. It would have been more than enough if Jesus Christ would have given a poor soul permission to love him. But that he should love us, and woo us to love him, and take pains to make us believe that he does love us, this is transcendent love! O! believers, such is the strength and transcendency of the love of Christ towards you, that when he was upon earth, he made it his great work to not only share his love freely, but to persuade you to believe it fully. And now that he is gone to heaven, he has taken care to appoint ambassadors who always in his name urge you to believe that he loves you. And it is the great longing of his soul to fill you, not only with his own love, but with his Father's love too. Wherever the gospel of free grace is preached, the message is this: that God so loved the world that he sent his son. And that Jesus Christ himself so loved poor souls that he came. And that if any would but believe, they might have him, and in him enjoy everlasting life and the fullness of divine love.

To all this I might add the consideration of the easy price that Jesus Christ sets upon his love which he offers. This investment into his love is mere acceptance of him. If any man will come to the fountain of love, he may partake of the waters freely. That fountain is not sealed, but rather a perpetual, open fountain. And this is the transcendency of his love, that it is open, even for those in whom there was a fountain of wrath and enmity flowing up against him. O my brethren! When you consider that the love of Christ is in every way full and free in its offering, and that he offers rich love to those who by nature were the children of wrath, certainly you must conclude that the love of Christ is a transcendent love that it passes knowledge. David describes the special love he shared with Jonathan as "wonderful, passing the love of women," (2 Sam. 1:26). Surely, believers, the love of Christ to you is transcendently wonderful, not only passing the love of women, but also the love shared between Jonathan and David. It is greater than any or all the loves of all the creatures of all time. Neither man nor angels could, or ever did, express so much love as Jesus Christ has not only expressed and declared but continues to urge souls to accept. I shall add nothing more to demonstrate such love but this, that when I have said all that I can of the love of Christ, you will have reason to tell me that the half was not told you. For the love of Christ is such that all the saints who enjoy it in the fullest measure, are unable to express it, and so wrap up their souls in wondering at it and cry that it is a love passing knowledge.

Before I come to the application, I shall briefly answer two objections which may be made against the truth of this doctrine.

Objection 1: If the love of Christ is transcendent to believers, why does he often allow their enemies to triumph over them and insult them? Surely will not the weak believer say, "if Christ loves me so highly, why does he permit me to lie so low? If I am so near to his heart, how is it that he allows wicked men to tread upon me? If he holds me in his heart, why does he allow me to lie at the world's feet?"

Answer 1: This act may co-exist with love. For example, Christ is dearly beloved of the Father, and yet the Father permitted wicked men to persecute him. You can surely not suffer worse than he did, and yet he was beloved of the Father, and that in a transcendent manner. In like manner, you may be the beloved of Christ's soul and still be delivered into the hands of your enemies (Jer. 12:7).

2.) This is not only consistent with love, but it is also an act of love. For while Christ permits these sufferings of yours, he makes you like himself. This situation is desired of Paul, as it makes him conformable to Christ (Phil. 3:10). Even a mourning garment is glorious when it is the same garment that Christ wears. What soul is there that may not be proud and glory in its tribulations, if he considers that in them, he is made like Christ?

Objection 2: Some will object further and say, "I do not question whether Christ loves me transcendently because of the sufferings I am under, but rather because of the desertions in which I am in. Alas! I question whether he loves me at all, because he withdraws himself from me so long. I have much more reason to question whether he loves me transcendently when I see him deny me his company altogether. I will not deny that he smiles sweetly, but I am a stranger to those smiles. There was a time when I thought he loved me transcendently, but now I fear he does not love me at all, for he deserts me all too often."

Answer 2: To those who fear Christ has deserted them, I would say but three words.

First, when you feel that Christ has withdrawn himself from you, this feeling is only in show, not in substance. When the sun does not shine, it is absent in show. However, it is still present behind a cloud. I have often thought that Christ's withdrawing, in this respect, may be called his concealed presence rather than his real absence. He was close by Mary, though she did not see him. He was in the company of his disciples, though they did not know him. His presence was not manifest, not because his person was not there but because their eyes were blinded that they did not know him (Luke 24:16).

Secondly, these withdrawings are not complete. Christ never so withdrew from the believer without leaving something behind, ("My beloved put in his hand by the hole of the door, and my bowels were moved for him," (Song 5:4). And surely, his hand was never empty. If he is absent in shining, he is present in strengthening; though he does not appear rich in love, yet he is still present, upholding your life. The very breath you breathe declares that Christ is present in some measure. If Jesus were not within your heart, you would not hunger after him. These desires for him are demonstrations that in some measure he is with you still.

Thirdly, Christ's withdrawing will not be final. He will be found again, even if he is not felt now. And when he returns, he will make rich amends for his absence. After experiencing such a desertion, Mr. Peacock exclaimed, "the sea is not more full of water, nor the sun more full of light, than my heart is full of joy, the joy that I feel in my heart is incredible!" Another believer, after experiencing spiritual drought, joyously announced, "Ah, he is come, he is come, he has kissed me with the kisses of his lips, his love is better than wine, he has not deceived me, neither will he deceive any."

Though believers give Christ occasion to go away quite often, Christ never goes away altogether, for even in his supposed absence, his presence is concealed, and once the time of withdrawing is complete, he makes rich amends for his going away. What do these experiences declare, but that his love is transcendent, passing knowledge.

Four words I shall add by way of application, namely, 1.) information, 2.) reproof, 3.) exhortation, and, 4.) persuasion.

First, for information, in as much as it is clear that Christ loves his own with transcendent love, then it may inform us of these four things.

The first is regarding the matter of that great and dreadful curse which Paul denounces against those who do not love Christ, "If any man love not the Lord Jesus, let him be anathema, maranatha," (1 Cor. 16:22). That is, let him be cursed with the highest and greatest degree of cursing that may be possible. For of those three degrees of cursing, which the Jews used in their threefold excommunication, that of *anathema maranatha* was the highest; and it includes this: let the Lord come and strike this person with eternal perdition. And tell me, do not those expose themselves to this dreadful curse who do not love such a one as Jesus Christ is, who loves his own with a transcendent love? Mind this, you who do not love the Lord Jesus, what can you say for yourselves, that you should not lie under this curse? Why do you not love Jesus Christ? What reason have you for it? Is he not lovely, fairer than the sons of men? Is he not loving? Does not his love to his own pass the love of women? Were Christ unkind, you might have cause to plead with some pretense that you have reason not to love him; but being so kind, so loving that he opens his heart and lets out transcendent love to all that are his, certainly you may expect, and that justly, to be accursed for not loving Christ.

Secondly, you see here the true ground of a believer's glory. Is it not glorious to be beloved of Christ with such a transcendent love as you have heard? Well may believers make their boast of Christ all day long, and well may they glory in the love that they enjoy. For that love is transcendent, passing knowledge. None of all the sons or daughters of men have any such just ground of glory, though they enjoy the love of all the creatures, as believers have, who enjoy only the love of Christ. For that love they have in him infinitely transcends and excels all that love which any can have from all the creatures. Let the world falsely and fondly brag of their creature-loves, while you rejoice with joy exceedingly great and full of glory. For having the love of Christ, you have that love which passes knowledge.

And surely, believers, if the men of the world think they have sufficient ground to glory in this, that they enjoy the love of some great men, you have much more ground to rejoice who enjoy this high love of him who is indeed greater than all. Do men think they have just ground to sit and glory in that they sip the puddle drops of creatures loves? Do you not have more greater ground that is just and true, to sing and glory in the fact that you drink in the pure love of Jesus Christ which is so sweet, so excellent, and so transcendent, as that it passes knowledge?

Thirdly, the truth that Christ loves believers with a transcendent love is the foundation for all that he does for them. You may wonder how it is that Christ does so much for you. He fills you with his unsearchable riches, he crowns you with his own glory, he gives you choice gifts, and he showers you with choice graces. He embraces your souls in his arms until you are ready to cry out. Why does Christ do all this for me? When you are sick, he visits you and sits by your bed. When you go abroad, Christ walks with you. You lean on him as your beloved. When you are in the wilderness, he comes to you. And if you are in prison, he visits you there. All this makes you cry out, "why should my Lord come to me like this?"

O believer, it is because he loves you with a transcendent love! All that he does for you, all that he gives you, all that he bestows on you, is because his love is beyond understanding. You may wonder why Christ sanctifies such unsanctified hearts as your own, and why he cleanses by the washing of the water of his word such an impure spirit as you have. You may ponder why the Lord of glory should stoop to wash such a creature as you are. It is because Christ loves you with a transcendent love. Christ does everything he does for you because of his transcendent love for you.

Fourthly, because Christ loves you with such a transcendent love, you have just ground to build your faith upon him. Why do you doubt whether Christ will do this for you, or give that to you, when he loves you with such a transcendent love? Upon all occasions, exercise your faith in your beloved. Whatever it is that you need, whatever it is that you would have, believe that Christ will not let you go without it. For why would he? He loves you with a transcendent love. Let us now look at three cases in which believers can exercise their faith on the assurance of Christ's transcendent love.

First is the case of hearing their prayers. Surely, he that so transcendently loves them will without a doubt hears their prayers. You have great necessities, you say. You also say that Christ is always able to help you. And yet you wonder if he will hear you when you pray. Should you not believe that he will, when you consider the transcendent love he bears to you? The love that is in his heart towards you will open his ears to hear the breathings that come from you. Indeed, sometimes he may seem to be deaf and not hear your prayers. But it is to try your faith. For he will hear you and accept you regarding whatever you desire according to his will that is for your good, that he may declare his transcendent love. You know Christ called the woman of Canaan a "dog," and seemed to speak harsh to her. And yet even all the while his heart was burdened for her, and there was love in his heart toward her. And though he seemed to deny her request for a while that he might try the sincerity of her faith, yet afterwards he granted her request that he might declare the reality of his own love. Therefore, you may be assured that in this case you have a sure ground of faith, O believers. Christ will not reject your prayers because he loves you, and the more transcendent his love is toward you, the surer you may be that he will hear you.

Secondly is the case of obtaining counsel from Christ and knowing the mind of Christ. This point will inform us of a sure ground of faith and love. Love will open Christ's heart, allowing you to see the counsels that are there. You say you would love to know the mind of Christ concerning this or that. But you doubt that he will ever open his mind to you about the one or the other? Why do you doubt that he would, O believer? Is not his transcendent love sufficient ground for the acting of your faith? Truly, because his heart is toward you, therefore it will be with you, (Judges 16:15). Delilah said to Samson, "How can you say, 'I love you,' when your heart is not with me?" You have no reason to say such a thing to the Lord. You can be assured that his heart will be with you because you know that he loves you. I persuade my own heart, and yours also, to this point, to seek Christ regarding the truth of a particular scripture or the answer to some question. Because Christ loves you, act in faith to believe that in due time he will reveal his mind to you in both the one and the other.

Thirdly, Christ's transcendent love gives a sure ground of faith in the case of assisting your fellow saints in their time of suffering. As Christ who loves you in such a transcendent manner will not let you always be under times of great sufferings, for he sympathizes with you in all your afflictions. He looks at your sufferings as his own. Because he loves you with a transcendent love, with this same love he will pull you out of your sufferings. Upon this ground of Christ's transcendent love, exercise a sweet and singular faith that he will soon deliver you out of sufferings. As he will not always strive with you, so neither will he always allow wicked men to trample on you. The truth that Christ loves his own with a transcendent love may justly reprove the world and the saints themselves also.

First, it may reprove the world, that is, those who think that Christ is an austere man (Luke 19:21). Christ, you see, is not austere but sweet. His name, as well as his nature, is love. Be reproved, those who entertain reviling and unkind thoughts of Christ. You wrong him in his love, and yourselves in the truth, when you think that he is not a loving Lord; you shall before long not only see that he loves, but that he loves all his own with a love passing knowledge.

But secondly, it reproves the saints also, who are ready very often to question, if not the reality, still the transcendency, of Christ's love. Be reproved for saying that Christ does not love you at all, or if he does, he only loves you very little. I profess that it is sad to see upon what petty, poor occasions even believers themselves are ready to question at least the greatness of Christ's love. If he denies them something they want, something that their heart is set upon so much, they think that his heart is not set upon them at all. They propose that Christ only loves them a little because he does not give them what they think they want so badly. Your hearts, O believers, will tell you the particulars of your own in this case, and therefore I pass them by. Only let the word of reproof fall upon you, who for any occasion, whether great or small, dare to question the transcendency of Christ's love.

Thirdly, upon consideration of this transcendent love which Christ bears to them, this should exhort believers to do at least these four things.

First, tremble to think that you should ever sin against him who loves you so much. View your sins in the light of your Savior's love; and when you see the transcendency of that love which is in his heart towards you, then sit down and grieve your great sins against him. His transcendent love does its sweet work in your spirit when the thoughts of it make you mourn for your sins. For the present, I will not dispute whether mourning for sin before closing with Christ can be sincere. But I am sure of this, that after closing with Christ and tasting of his love, then mourning for sin is most sweet. And though nothing in the world can melt the heart for sin, thoughts of the love of Christ will. Let his love have such a work in your hearts then. O! let his transcendent love, written with the blood of his heart, dissolve your adamant spirit. And let it make you mourn for your sins greatly. "They shall see him whom they have pierced, and mourn," (Zech. 12:10). When you see him whom you have pierced with your sins, do you not mourn, especially when you see him in the light of love? I say no more but this, either you have not tasted this transcendent love of Christ, or else your spirits are hardened, if the sense and thoughts of his love do not cause you to mourn for your sin. Let this word of exhortation sink deeply into your hearts (O believers!) Weep tears of blood to think that ever you should sin against Jesus Christ, who has written in his own blood this truth, that he loves you with a love passing knowledge.

Secondly, I urge you to be ambitious to answer this transcendent love of your Savior, with a similar love. Let this love of your Lord magnetize your love for him; let it constrain you to love him transcendently, who loves you so. I know it is impossible to parallel it. But you can strive to at least imitate it. Do not content yourself to love him little that loved you much. Seeing that Christ has loved you richly, be ashamed to love him poorly. Ambition in this respect will be a grace if Christ's love to you inflames you to love him greatly. Be ambitious to declare as much love to him as is possible in you, for this is the love he gives you.

The philosopher Mirandola (1463-1494) notes that it is a badge of love if one is willing and even desirous to suffer for their beloved. Believers, Christ's love to you had such a work as that, and if your love to him has not yet risen so high as to desire to suffer for him, let it at least rise high enough to be willing to suffer anything he calls you to suffer, for that will be a sweet and sure character of love.

Paul says that the love of Christ *constrains* us, (2 Cor. 5:14). The consideration of Christ's love holds a constraining power upon our spirit, such that if Christ died for us, we should be willing to die for Christ. A Christian is sweetly exercised when the golden ball of divine love is tossed between Christ's heart and his. Let this therefore sink into your spirits, labor to answer this transcendent love of Christ towards you, this love which passes knowledge.

Thirdly, upon all occasions, know that you have recourse to this transcendent love. Believers, though the world deride you, you can take refuge in this love of Christ to comfort you when you come home. Look into Christ's heart and there see that which is better than gold, which is to say his grace. Weak people have their little bottles of spirits and cordials to carry about with them, to refresh them when they are faint. Believers, especially those who are weak, imitate their wisdom. Let this bottle of Christ's transcendent love always be in your heart and have recourse to this. Refresh your spirits upon all occasions (especially when you grow faint), for without doubt, there is refreshing power in this transcendent love of Christ to keep your hearts from fainting under troubles. Jesus Christ in his trouble had recourse to his Father's love. Why then, in any trouble, do you not have recourse to Christ's love?

Fourthly, make it your concern to imitate your Savior. Love all his as he does, with a transcendent love. Beloved, if Christ loved us, we ought then to love one another, and that very dearly. Be followers of Christ as dear children, and walk in love one to another, as Christ has loved you all. Whoever they are that are believers, Christ loves them very dearly, because they are his. If he does, why shouldn't you? Wherever you see the light of Christ's love shining upon any heart, cause your love to shine also upon the same. Especially take heed that you do not frown on those on whom Christ smiles. As Christ loves all his with a transcendent love, whoever they be that belong to Jesus Christ let them have your love also, if for no other reason than because Christ is in them. Learn to love them truly because you know that Christ loves them transcendently. Christ loves all saints, no matter how different they are from each other, with the same love. No matter what differing opinions they have, and even if they err in their understanding of some truths, they are all the object of Christ's affection. It is sad, indeed, when some believers do not look on other believers with affection, for all are beloved of Jesus Christ. How can one believer look on another believer with a frowning countenance when Christ looks on him with a smiling face? Do not allow unbelievers to see you, you who are highly beloved of Jesus Christ, belittling and reviling one another. I say no more but this, seeing as Christ loves every believer with a transcendent love, we should do likewise.

Fourthly, I shall add but a word of persuasion to persuade all those who are strangers to Jesus Christ to come in unto him. O that you could behold the glorious beams of transcendent love towards all believers! There is no doubt but such a sight as that would work on your heart and draw your spirit to close with him, who is so lovely in himself, and so loving to those who wander up and down the wilderness of the world. Return, sinner, to the son. Embrace Jesus Christ. Know that he is the Lord of love who embraces all that come to him freely and loves them all transcendently.

It may be that your ignorance of this is keeping you from closing with him; but know it now, and be persuaded to come to Christ; to close with him, to embrace his gospel, to love his truth, to be conversant in his ordinances, knowing that if you do, you shall have this love from him which *passes knowledge*. Be contented now to break off from the ways of sin and vanity and come into the ways of righteousness. Do not say if you take up Christ in his gospel and in his ways, that friends will leave you and the world will hate you, and the devil will stir up the sons of Satan against you. It does not matter if men turn away from you and leave you alone, for Christ will embrace you. Though they hate you, Christ will love you. And why should you fear the sons of Satan when you enjoy the love of Christ's heart? Give ear, O children of folly. Be wise, and you shall taste love. Christ calls you all, whoever you are, to come to him, embrace him lovingly, and you shall find him loving you transcendently. I have said all, if I can persuade you to be drawn to Jesus Christ with these cords of love.

No matter if you are a stranger to it now, if you will but come in, you shall know the love of Christ and the truth of this point. Your own experience should be forced to witness this, that Jesus Christ loves believers with a transcendent love that passes knowledge.

Sermon 5

"And to know the love of Christ, which passes knowledge, that ye might be filled with all the fullness of God," (Eph. 3:19).

There is nothing of greater force to allure men than the desire for knowledge. Job tells us that vain men desire to be wise. Since the fall we are subject to folly, and in that sense we are vain. Yet there remains some mindfulness in us that recognizes the value of knowledge and desires to be wise. But here is our misery, there is a great deal of vanity in our desire for knowledge. We are all apt to desire the knowledge that is above us, that which is unattainable. It was this golden apple of knowledge which so tempted our grandmother Eve. Although the best that she got by eating that apple was the knowledge of evil, she was still drawn to eat the apple because it was both pleasant to the taste and desirable to make one wise. And surely, as our grandmother ate those sour grapes, so all her children have ever since had our teeth set on edge with the same desire.

All too often, out of an eager desire and affection for knowledge, we are apt to pry into those hidden secrets which God has not revealed. But as the apostle says, "I will show you a more excellent way," by declaring how you may pursue knowledge, so that you should neither reach too high nor stoop too low in seeking it. For who shall ascend to bring down Jesus Christ from above and to reveal the knowledge of hidden glories and inconceivable mysteries? And who shall descend to raise him up from beneath? Rather, remember the Scripture is near, even the gospel which we preach. Labor to know this gospel, and you shall know enough, not only regarding salvation but also to the perfection of your knowledge.

Christ, who is the wisdom of God and in whom are hidden all the treasures of wisdom and knowledge, is fully and clearly revealed in the gospel. By studying to gain knowledge of it, we shall come to the knowledge of him. Of all knowledge, the knowledge of Christ is most sacred, so it is most satisfactory. And of all things in Christ, the knowledge of his love is the most satisfactory, so it is most sweet. It is this knowledge which the apostle here prays that the Ephesians might obtain. It does not matter whether you know arts and sciences, though in themselves they are important and hold value. Neither does it concern you to be acquainted with other truths of the Scriptures, which in their place are very precious. But what does concern you is that you know the love of Christ passes knowledge.

Our third point to be spoken from these words is this, that it is necessary for every Christian to know the transcendent love of Jesus Christ.

We have already endeavored to hold out, at least, a beam of light towards the discovery of that heart-love that is in Christ towards his own. And at this time my desire is to hint at something which may at least put you on to endeavor to make a further discovery of the riches, and the glory, and the transcendency of that love. For my design is to make it appear that the study for the knowledge of his love is a very choice, special, and necessary concern for you all.

Now, when I say that the knowledge of the love of Christ is of necessary concern, I do not mean the bare believing of this truth, but a clear and full understanding of its substance and circumstances. There are divine and infinite dimensions in the love of Christ, and it is our duty to labor for the knowledge of all of these. We should strive to be able to measure both the length and the breadth, and to scale the height and to sound the depth of the love of Christ.

Christ's heart is a very glorious mine of love, and it beckons us to dig very deep into it and not content ourselves with a bare discovery of that golden ore, or vein of love, which is at the top of the mine and in which we may easily discover in the very letter of the gospel. Rather, it calls us to attain to the deep, mysterious discoveries which saints by the light of the Spirit come to attain.

We should also endeavor to gain an experiential knowledge of this love. As the painter curiously painted love by depicting it out of his own heart, so we may be able by our Christian discourses to demonstrate and declare what the love of Christ is from the experience of it in our own hearts. Divines observe that the Scriptures do not support any saving knowledge of Christ that is not experiential. And certainly, the knowledge of the love of Christ ought to be not only a head knowledge, but a heart knowledge, an experiential knowledge.

To apprehend the knowledge of the love of Christ more clearly, we should first note that this knowledge is of extreme importance. There are many things that may be expedient to know, but none are of such importance as the love of Christ. This knowledge is not only expedient for us to know; it is also of the utmost importance.

Secondly, some knowledge may be of accidental importance and yet not of necessary importance. However, information that is accidental to the discovery of some greater truth has an added layer of necessity placed upon it.

Thirdly, the knowledge of Christ's love is of necessary importance for every Christian. Some truths may be of necessary importance for some persons who are anointed with a higher anointing and employed in a more special way (as officers in the church, *etc.*). But this knowledge we speak of is of necessary importance for every soul that is named by the name of Christ. And especially every soul that is united to Jesus Christ ought to labor for a solid knowledge of the love of Christ. As the fathers in Christ's school are not above this knowledge, neither are the babes and children in Christ's school beneath it. Rather, all are necessarily bound, and the responsibility lies upon them all to gain some understanding of the love of Christ which passes knowledge.

I will add one word by way of caution; I do not say, neither would I have you think, that this is the only knowledge to be labored for. Indeed, it is the sovereign, but not the sole knowledge, which Christians should desire and endeavor to obtain.

Therefore, I am not saying you should gain this knowledge exclusively, shutting out other truths, but as inclusively, and eminently driving at this in a peculiar manner. And as Christ said with reference to doing those things, you ought to have done that one especially, while not leaving the other undone. I say that regarding the knowledge of the love of Christ, you ought to labor for this diligently, as it is more special and of necessary importance. But at the same time, you should not neglect the knowledge of other gospel truths as if they were of no necessity or no importance at all.

For proof, I shall not need to add many Scriptures since it is so fully laid down here. Certainly, the wise apostle Paul would never have so earnestly and particularly begged of God that the Ephesians might know the love of Christ which passes knowledge if it was not of special and necessary importance for them. I shall only add to this his desire for the Ephesians, that determination of his for himself (which he expresses to the Corinthians), "I am determined not to know anything among you, save Jesus Christ and him crucified

(1 Cor. 2:2)." Now the knowledge of Jesus Christ crucified is the knowledge of Christ in his love.

His whole life was like one great sermon of love, yet the death of Christ was a longer, and clearer sermon of love than all his life was. Never did Christ speak love more fully and more freely than when he was on the cross. Now then, if Paul determined to know nothing but this, we may safely conclude, both from his determination for himself and his desire for the Ephesians, that the knowledge of Christ's transcendent love is of necessary importance for every Christian.

I shall offer some reasons to make this point yet clearer.

First, the knowledge of the love of Christ contains in it the sum of the gospel, as Christ is the sum of the gospel, and love the sum of Christ. God so loved the world that he gave Christ, and Christ so loved the world that he *gave* himself. And these truths contain in them the marrow and pith of all the gospel. This little word "love" (written in golden letters of free grace upon the heart of Jesus Christ) is an epitome of the gospel. Loving the Father fulfills the law, and loving Christ fulfills the gospel. You have done the law if you love God sincerely, and you understand the gospel if you know Christ's love soundly.

Secondly the knowledge of Christ's love is of necessary importance because it contains in it the highest motive to duty. You will obey with the sweetness that is in your own spirit and with that acceptance of God even if you do not act from a principle of love. The knowledge of the love of Christ is what chiefly enflames our love to him. When Israel was a child and did not understand this love, God taught him to go forward by taking him by the arm (Hosea 11:3). God demonstrated his love, but Israel did not understand. In like manner, we shall never walk in a way pleasing to God by simply doing our duty, if we do not better understand what this love is and how it is that Christ loves us.

Paul was more diligent than all the rest of the apostles in his labors. Surely, this might be the reason he understood more of the love of Christ than the rest did. The knowledge of Christ's love which Paul came to have was like a whole siege of motives for Paul, both to die and to suffer for Jesus Christ. There is no soul that doesn't need spurred to duty, being dull in himself. But the knowledge of the love of Christ, being of such special efficacy this way, must also be of necessary importance for every Christian.

Thirdly, Christ's love is the fountain of a believer's life, and therefore it is of necessary importance for a believer to know it, in as much as he cannot live without it. This is life eternal, to *know* the love of Christ which *passes knowledge*. If it is essential for the soul to live, it must also be of necessary importance to know Christ's love, because he cannot enjoy the one without the other. Paul says, "I live by the faith," (faith is simply a higher degree of knowledge of the love of Christ), "of the Son of God, who loves me." As Moses pressed the Israelites to the sincere keeping of the law, "for it is your life," in like manner may we urge Christians to the serious knowledge of Christ's love for it is our soul's life.

Fourthly, the knowledge of Christ's love is the foundation of a soul's joy and the Christian's comfort, and therefore of such necessary importance. The reason why the saints are sometimes so sad is because they do not know the love of Christ, at least in all its dimensions. For this reason, peace is joined with love. "Peace and love from God the Father, and our Lord Jesus Christ," (Eph. 6:23). The hearts of believers will be at peace if they fully *understand* the love of Christ. Indeed, they live sweetly in Christ's love because they have it, but as they think, "I go sadly in my lack of Christ's love, because I think there is none for me." The soul is sad when it does not see the fullness of the love of Christ.

Another soul may say, "One who has less sin than I have may live joyfully because of Christ's love, but I must go sadly because I fear he will not love me." The reason for this soul's sadness is because it does not know the fullness of love that is in Christ and the freedom from it. For without a doubt, if we only knew the love of Christ better than we do, we should not be sad as often as we are. That disciple John who knew much of the love of Jesus, and had declared the knowledge of it to others, said it was for this end: "These things I write unto you that your joy might be full." Seeing that the joy and comfort of our souls is built upon the love of Christ as its foundation, it urges us to gain its knowledge.

Fifthly, the knowledge of Christ's love is of necessary importance because it gives rise to Christian thankfulness. Thankfulness springs from this fountain of Christ's love. Those souls most thankful for the love of Christ are those who understand it most; ignorance begets ingratitude, but knowledge makes thankful. "Bless the Lord, o my soul, and forget not all his benefits!" Men will not be thankful for what they forget; neither can men remember what they do not know. All that Christ looks for from the saints is that they acknowledge the transcendent love he bears unto them. We will never be able to sing glory and dominion to him who has loved us except we know how he loved us. Look how the lark, at the discovery of the light of the day, ascends chirping and chirping; and the lighter the heavens appear, the higher she ascends, and the sweeter she sings. In like manner, the soul, who knows the love of Christ and sees the light of his love, mounts and sings, and the more brightly the beams of Christ's heart love shines in on them, the higher the soul is elevated and the sweeter it sings that spiritual song of thankfulness to Christ. You are bound, believers, to thank Christ for his love, and you will never desire to cancel that bond as long as you know the transcendency of that love with which he has bound you.

Christ's love is the legacy he has left Christians. Surely it is of necessary importance for Christians to know what Christ left them in his will. He has not left them ample possessions nor stately buildings in this world, but rather dear love, rich love, transcendent love, love passing knowledge. This is what Christ has left to believers. "As the Father has loved me, so have I loved you," (John 1:5).

Ask the widow whether it concerns her to know what her husband left her. Ask the child whether it is necessary to know what his father left him, and they both will say "yes!" Why believers, your everlasting Father and your soul's husband, Jesus Christ, has left you nothing but his love. Surely it is necessary that you should know it.

Next, as the soul is filled with the knowledge of the love of Christ, so it is filled with the fullness of God. You empty creatures, does it not concern you to be filled with divine fullness, the fullness of God? Surely you will say, "yes!" Then know that you should be well acquainted with the love of Christ, for without that you cannot be so filled.

Some have thought that knowledge is nothing but a union between the object and the understanding. Therefore, they conclude that as God is love, and the knowledge of God's love is the union with the soul, then certainly, by knowing the one, we partake and are filled with the other. Observe how the apostle therefore joins these two in the text – to know the love of Christ which passes knowledge, "that you may be filled with all the fullness of God." Every drop of this knowledge of the love of Christ tends toward filling the soul with the fullness of God. Surely therefore to be filled, and to be filled with all the fullness of God and the knowledge of Christ's love so advantageous, must needs be a thing of special importance for every Christian to labor to know.

Briefly now let us turn to *application*. Notwithstanding the fact that the knowledge of the love of Christ is essential, it has been little studied. Men have been very diligent to search after other truths, but slow in searching after the knowledge of Christ's love. An ample discovery of this love of Christ may well be pursued by those who desire to study the divines, but it has been little handled by others. Indeed, much of the law has been discovered, but little of the gospel, (especially in this point of Christ's love). I do not know any one author of eminency who has purposed to study and discourse concerning the transcendency of the love of Christ.

Surely it is very sad to think that the knowledge of the love of Christ, being of such necessary and high importance, has been so little inquired into. What a gallant challenge it would be for someone who is acquainted with the Spirit in a large measure to review the whole history of the gospel in order to observe the glorious shining examples of the love of Christ to believers. It would be precious if some would take it in hand and perfect it to that purpose. But it is sad to think it has been neglected so long and gives us cause to lament.

Secondly, we may lament not only because this knowledge has only been studied slightly, but especially because that after all Christ did to show us this love, very little is gained. We may weep to think how little of the love of Christ those who have pursued it have realized. In Revelation we read of a book that was sealed, and John wept bitterly because no man was found worthy in heaven or in earth to open the book or to look thereon. Beloved, the heart of Christ may be compared to a glorious book in which the mysterious history of his transcendent love is written. But alas! Who is able to open this book to discover its mysteries?

When we come to heaven, we shall then be in a state of more perfect knowledge of the love of Christ. But alas! Even then we shall never be able to comprehend his love in its full perfection, that is, as fully as it may be known. Indeed, then we shall apprehend it in the perfection of our knowledge, in so far as it can be known by the finite knowledge of creatures.

Without a doubt, there shall be a fullness of knowledge of Christ according to the utmost bounds to which our knowledge, when it is perfected to the highest, is capable of. Yet when it is considered, in regard to all the effects and purposes where that knowledge extends itself, I think that through all eternity we shall be admiring and adoring this love of Christ which passes knowledge.

We must consider that while the knowledge of the love of Christ is of necessary importance, it has been little pursued by many; and even when we make the greatest effort to search after it, we shall never be able fully to attain it. This is lamentable indeed.

This truth may also be useful in reproving those who neglect to study the knowledge of the love of Christ altogether. Few men diligently study the Bible, and less study the light and luster and glory of the gospel, the love of Christ to believers. And I cannot help but think those blame-worthy who in these times flaunt their abilities to hammer out some of the more controversial truths of Scripture, and yet neglect the study of his love which is of such necessary importance. I do not altogether blame those who study the headship of Christ; yet to study the head of Christ, while neglecting his heart – to mind his government and yet neglect his love – is without doubt, a thing to be reproved.

But much more are those to be reproved who study neither the one, nor the other, but spend all their time and energies in controversies and niceties. They busy themselves with needless questions while neglecting this one necessary thing, namely, the knowledge of the love of Christ. These men resemble travelers on a journey who have good bread with them but choose rather to gnaw on hard stones. So it is with men who have the bread of life, Christ's love, when they neglect it and instead spend their time gnawing on hard trivium or at best, less than useful questions. Be reproved, you who spend your energy obtaining superfluous knowledge while neglecting to study the knowledge of Christ's love, which is of greatest importance.

Lastly, we shall add a word of exhortation to stir believers to study the love of Christ. You who have spent, or rather misspent many a precious hour reading romances and fond histories of feigned loves, yea, you who spend all your time with some matters of importance, but still neglecting this; be stirred up now to devote yourselves to the study of that which is sweet and necessary, namely the study of the love of Christ which passes knowledge.

You must understand that my desire is that you labor to be well versed students in this business. I would not have you content yourselves with generalities but labor to make a particular discovery of the love of Christ in its substance, its circumstances, and its various actions and declarations. And remember that this knowledge includes in it all that knowledge which is necessary to be known for salvation.

When you have studied it well, you shall find that there is nothing in the whole doctrine of salvation which is not comprehended in this love of Christ. As Calvin has well observed, this knowledge is both *safe* and *sweet;* it is not the kind of knowledge that will puff up the head; this knowledge *purifies* the heart. I do not doubt that anyone can stray in the paths of sin who attains to any spiritual saving degree of this knowledge. The love of Christ will constrain you to duty, and restrain you from sin; therefore, devote yourselves to this study above all others.

Now I shall offer some means to help you and motives to encourage you. But first a word of caution: be careful that you do not promise yourselves too much. In other words, do not think that you shall ever come to some level of perfect knowledge in this point, at least while you are in this life. It is a point which may take up the whole of your study, as the apostle notes in the 18th verse of this chapter, "that you may be able to comprehend with all saints." Some doctrines require the abilities and efforts of many scholars who then together may be able to make a good discovery. Such is the love of Christ, as that all the saints may well spend themselves in the study of it, and when they have brought all their notes together, and added all their studies together, they will realize they can only scratch the surface. Therefore, take heed of promising yourselves perfection in this study.

Now I add one more caution, not to deter you from the study but to make you more serious in it, and also to keep you from casting it off after you have begun to understand it. Some saints, as well as some scholars, after having made some progress in this study, find the business so hard and so high that they can never come to its perfect knowledge. They then begin to slack in their endeavors, and to eventually leave it alone altogether. But now beloved, consider it beforehand, that you may not afterwards leave the study of the love of Christ, because when you have spent yourselves to the uttermost, you shall never come to a perfect knowledge.

In addition, remember that the least beams of the love of Christ have so much light in them that they will be very sweet, and every piece or part of this knowledge will be of very special worth. For this reason, the low and imperfect knowledge of the love of Christ (if experiential and spiritual) is of infinitely more value than the high and perfect knowledge of ten thousand things besides.

Let me add one more note: that it is possible for you to attain to a very sweet and satisfactory degree of this knowledge. But what, you may ask, shall I do to attain a satisfactory degree of this knowledge of the love of Christ, so that I may be able to say, as it is in the text, that the love of Christ passes knowledge?

For that I shall offer you some directions concerning the means and how you may obtain the knowledge of the love of Christ and also, concerning the manner in which we should carry ourselves in that study.

For the means, I shall name these particulars.

First, be diligent in reading the gospel. The Bible in general gives testimony concerning the person of Jesus Christ, and also in some measure concerning his affection to the saints. But the gospel demonstrates the love of Christ to believers in a more ample, clear, and satisfactory way. That which all the prophets spoke of him, or of his love, is so allegorical that it is not as easy (at least for everyone) to observe the light of Christ's love so clearly shining in them. Although the sunshine of Christ's love is depicted throughout the Old Testament, it is more clouded and veiled there. But in the expanse of the New Testament, it shines in its full brightness, luster, and glory. For this reason, I urge you to read and study the gospel more energetically. And while doing so, be sure to remember that all that you shall read there, either about the life or death of Christ, is to be understood as a demonstration of his love to believers.

Secondly, if you would know the love of Christ, be sure to labor to get *into the heart* of Christ. That soul who knows little of Christ's love in its power and sweetness and spirituality, knows only Christ in his head. And without the knowledge of Christ in his heart, he is still a stranger to his love. Labor therefore to have Christ revealed in you; otherwise, all the knowledge which you have of the love of Christ will be of little to no purpose. Jesus Christ knows the Father most, because, as Scripture says, he lay in the Father's heart. In like manner labor to be in the heart of Jesus Christ, that you may better experience his love to believers.

Thirdly, consult with believers. Ask those objects of his love about the love of Christ to them. They that have experience of his love can best inform you. I have no doubt that a poor believer who has tasted the love of Christ, and in some measure experienced the transcendent sweetness of it, is far better able to help you in this great study of the love of Christ than the greatest scholar in the world who has read of his love, but yet has no experience of it in his soul.

Fourthly, study your own experiences. Consider how Christ has dealt particularly with your own soul. Remember how long he waited for you while you were still in sin and at enmity with him. How long did he stand knocking at the door before you opened it for him? How long did he woo your soul before you embraced him? How many ways did he undertake to work on you, to encourage you to open your heart to let him in, that he might love you? How freely did he show love to your soul? Was there any other condition on which he shared himself with you other than your acceptance of him? Did he not say when he came and knocked at your door, that if you would open the door, he would come in and sup with you? Did he not say, come and drink if you thirst? Come and drink, and if your heart is willing, partake of me and live forever? Mind those experiences of Christ's love towards you. Remember all the feasts of love which he has given you, and by these you will come to see how good, how kind, and how loving he is.

Lastly, add prayer to all these. It is the choicest wisdom to be wise in the knowledge of Christ's love. And if you lack this wisdom, James gives you his advice, "ask it of God," and if you ask God for a wise heart in this matter, he will not deny you, for he gives liberally to those who ask. Then ask of him much, beg of him a wise and understanding heart to know the love of Christ which passes knowledge. Intreat God that you may be taught of him, to know the love of God and of his son. As Christ said, every man that has heard and learned of the Father comes to me. So, every soul that the Father teaches will quickly learn to know the love of Christ to believers. And that you may be able to know the love of Christ in its luster, beg of God to bestow his Spirit on you. Christ has said that the Father will give the Spirit to him that asks him; and the apostle said that no man knows the things of a man, but the spirit of a man which is in him; so none can know the things of Christ, but the Spirit of Christ.

Go to the Lord Jesus and remind him of his promise. Tell him that he has promised to send his Spirit, and that when the spirit is come, he shall show Christ to the soul. Intreat him to show his Spirit, and intreat him also that his Spirit would come with the shedding abroad of his love. Ask that he would shed his love abroad into your heart, that you may be able with all saints to comprehend the height, and the depth, and the length, and the breadth of the love of Christ, and that you may be able also to know that love which passes knowledge!

Having thus given some of the means by which we may attain the knowledge of Christ's love, I shall now add a word or two concerning how we should behave ourselves in the use of this means, while we study the knowledge of Christ's love.

First, be very exact. Precision is requisite in all studies, but especially in this. Gather up all the crumbs and filings of the gold of Christ's love. When you read anything concerning Christ, observe the smiles of his countenance, the words of his lips, the gesture of his hands, the turning of his eye, as love observes them all.

Be very curious to study love in all its circumstances, in all its doings, in all its demonstrations. If ever you show precision in any study, show it in this. The more exact you are in this study, the clearer you will be able to comprehend Christ's love.

Secondly, be loving. Those know most of Christ's love to them who abound most in love to him. John seems to be most loving of all the disciples, and therefore he seems to have the greatest knowledge of Christ's love. Because he so desired to lean on the heart of the Lord Jesus, to him was revealed more than to the rest of the apostles. That man who expects mercy of God while being without mercy himself desires in vain to know Christ's love, for he is without love himself. You would do well to observe the context of this text in Ephesians 3:17-19. For the apostle said that you, "being rooted, and grounded in love, may be able to comprehend with all saints, what is the length, breadth, and depth, and height of the love of Christ, *etc.*" To be grounded in love is an excellent way to comprehend love. And doubtless, Christ will be very kind in the revelations of his love to those in whom he observes the workings of love.

Thirdly, be very admiring in all the study; let all your reading be mixed with admiration at every love passage of Christ. Sit and meditate at every word of love;

stay and wonder; adore the glory of that light which appears in any beam of love. And in the admiration of that love which does appear, cast yourself at the feet of Christ and cry out, "O the depth of love in thee! O the riches of the love of thy heart!"

Lastly, when you find yourself unable to comprehend the transcendency of this love, imitate the philosopher and cast yourself into that sea of love which you would attempt to fathom or sound, and yet are unable to. Let that love comprehend you, which you cannot comprehend yourself. Immerse and drown yourself in that vast ocean of your Savior's heart, and because you are not able with any measure to sound the depth, sink your very soul that it may be able to taste that which your study will not allow you to see.

I might add that all the time you spend in this study will be very delightful, and very profitable, and you will have no reason to regret any of it. Those who have misspent their time in reading the fine histories of feigned loves have at last been forced to confess their folly in so doing. That well-deserving author, Sir Philip Sidney, is reported to have lamented upon his deathbed that he misspent those gifts which God had given him in the penning of his well-written book, *Arcadia*. But surely for believers to lie on their deathbed and consider every hour spent in the study of Christ's love would be time you rejoice in.

Secondly, consider the times in which we live. How little love is there in these days! Surely, the love of many has grown cold and is little practiced. Though many complain of the lack of love, and seem to force the exercise of love, yet where is the man that makes it the sweetness of his life to let others taste the sweetness of his love? Surely while there is such little love among men, it is even more essential that we study the love that is in Christ.

Thirdly, especially consider the sweetness that the knowledge of the love of Christ will bring to your soul in any case. Little do you know what comfort is wrapped up in the knowledge of Christ's love. How often does a thought of this revive the spirits of the fainting saints? With what composure of spirit is a believer able to behave himself in any tribulation when he is without the knowledge of the love of his Savior? Without the knowledge of this love, nothing will be sweet. But with the knowledge of his love, nothing can be bitter. And this is that which we shall come to as the last thing observed from these words, namely, to let you see how sufficient the love of Christ is for supporting believers in any tribulation.

Sermon 6

"And to know the love of Christ, which passes knowledge, that ye might be filled with all the fulness of God," (Eph. 3:19).

He that is skilled at all in the knowledge of the times may well see that these times in which we live are very sad. Calamity lies upon every creature; and woe has entered the stage of the world, bringing terror to all, even believers themselves. Almost all the sons of men are in mourning because of the misery we are all under.

In these times what can be more suitable to our thoughts than to consider that which may serve to support our spirits. Believers would be wise to resort to something that is able to keep them from buckling under these tribulations. Indeed, our Lord Jesus, out of the riches of his mercy, has prepared and provided rich and glorious support for those souls of his. And it is our duty (especially those who are ministers of the Lord Jesus) to help believers discover what our Lord has prepared. Therefore, I shall endeavor to imitate the great apostle Paul; to show myself a helper of your joy rather than a lord over your faith. Paul was much about the furtherance of the joy and comfort of believers. This is what he is driving at in these words on behalf of the Ephesians, unless the news of his troubles burden them to the point of causing them to faint. So he bows his knees to the Father of our Lord Jesus Christ, pleading with him to give them the knowledge of the love of Christ that so by it, their spirits may be kept from fainting, either at the news of his, or the fear of their own tribulations. Therefore, Paul prayed to God on behalf of the Ephesians that they might know the love of Christ which passes knowledge. We may observe from this doctrine that spiritual knowledge of the transcendency of Christ's love towards his own is of special efficacy to keep our hearts from fainting under any troubles.

I suppose you easily see both the foundation and the proof of this point in this place. However, in order that you may see both more clearly, let me mention these three things.

First, consider that the apostle supposes the Ephesians' hearts were apt to faint at their tribulations. In the 13th verse, his desire that they might *not faint* clearly intimates this. Indeed, the children of faith are not only prone to fear but are apt to faint in those fears.

Secondly, observe how his desire that they might not faint causes him to make his *request known to God in prayer*, that God would keep them from fainting. "For this cause I bow my knees to the Father of our Lord Jesus, that you might not faint." I bow my knee to him who alone can support your spirits.

Thirdly, consider, that among the rest of those things which he prays to God for on their behalf, he also asks that they may *know* the love of Christ which passes knowledge.

And indeed, the very spirit and strength of all that the apostle prayed for in the former verses on their behalf comes to rest in this last. This is, as it were, the last remedy the doctor has to give his patient. For if this fails, the doctor has nowhere else to go. In the same way, you may easily see that this text serves as a stronghold for this truth as well as solid proof of its substantial importance.

And yet, that you may see this truth more clearly, I will in a word show you how the very spirits and strength of the other blessings which he prayed for on their behalf are all wrapped up in this, namely, the knowledge of the love of Christ.

Consider that he first prayed that they might be strengthened in the inward man by his spirit (verse 16). Now what is that strength of the inward man by the spirit, but that divine and spiritual joy which is through him. The joy of the Lord gives strength (Neh. 8:10). Now it is easy to demonstrate that the chief ground on which the Holy Spirit builds that joy in the hearts of believers is the shedding abroad of the love of Christ in them. Christ promised to send his spirit as a comforter to believers, saying that "He," (*i.e.,* his Spirit) "shall take of mine and show it unto you," (John 16:15). Now what is there in all of our Lord Jesus Christ of sweeter efficacy and power which the spirit can take and declare to believers than his love which passes knowledge?

So, the strengthening of the inward man by the Holy Spirit helps support your soul from fainting.

Whether by blessing you with divine joy or bringing you divine comfort, his spirit reveals something of the heart of Christ to the hearts of believers for the strengthening of the inward man.

Secondly, as a means to keep the Ephesians from fainting, the apostle prays that Christ may "dwell in their hearts by faith," (verse 17). Now the strength of this comfort lies in the knowledge of Christ's love. But the soul may say, "yes, but will Christ dwell in my heart? I want to believe it, but what ground do I have for such a belief? He is the high and lofty one, and I am a poor creature. He is not only the brightness of his Father's glory, but the fulness of the Father's holiness. Will such a pure person as he is truly come and dwell in such a polluted house as I am?" Now all this reasoning is quieted, and this doubting easily resolved, by the knowledge of Christ's love. For he that knows the love of Christ knows how willingly Christ comes into the heart of a poor believer, and how that daily and even hourly he stands at the door knocking for entrance.

It is very plain that the knowledge of the love of Christ is of such special virtue and efficacy that it keeps the hearts of believers from fainting under tribulations. But I shall now demonstrate this point a little more, first, by discussing wherein this knowledge of the love of Christ consists. And then secondly, by showing where this special efficacy of that knowledge appears, for keeping the soul from fainting in the time of trouble.

And then in closing, I shall make some use and application.

Firstly, in what does the knowledge of Christ's love consist, or what kind of knowledge of the love of Christ keeps the heart from fainting?

In general, I hinted at it in that expression, "the spiritual knowledge of the love of Christ," *i.e.,* a knowledge of Christ's love that the soul has by the revelation of the Spirit shedding abroad that love on the spirit of a believer. As the carnal knowledge of Christ's person is not saving, neither is it sweet; so, neither is the carnal knowledge of his love. It is the spiritual knowledge of his person, and the spiritual knowledge of his love, which furthers the everlasting happiness of a soul hereafter, and the sweetness and comfort of a soul here.

More particularly, I will share two words for the clarification of what the knowledge of Christ's love is.

First, negatively it does not consist in its bare notion. All divine knowledge (whatever it is) is without any efficacy if it is nothing but the mere consideration of it. Regarding duty, knowledge is not sufficient to move the soul to doing unless it sinks deep into the marrow of that soul. As the parable of Christ shows, the word that fell among stones lacked the ability to take root and was unable to bear fruit. In like manner with reference to joy, even the knowledge of Christ's love cannot restore the soul unless it sinks down from the head into the hearts of believers. But as the apostle says, the knowledge of the glory of God the Father unto salvation is when God who commanded the light to shine out of darkness, "shines into their hearts," (2 Cor. 4:6). The virtue of the knowledge of the love of God causes the soul to be patient in waiting and, by consequence, not fainting in times of trouble. This is why God tells us to direct our hearts toward his love (2 Thess. 3:5). This is also how you may know that the knowledge of the love of Christ does not consist in merely the bare notion, or apprehension, of it in the head. It must be born in the heart.

The right knowledge of the love of Christ chiefly consists in two areas. First, in a particular application of the love of Christ to the soul by faith. That is, the soul should be able to apprehend to himself, in particular, the love of Christ which he understands to be available to every believer in general. The soul should be able to say of the love of Christ, "it is mine! For what is all this to me, if it is not mine?" Similarly, the soul may say, "what is it to me if a transcendent love in the heart of Christ to believers exists, if I do not have a share in it?" The preaching of the word does not profit those in whom it is not mixed with faith, *i.e.*, for those in whom it is not particularly applied to the heart. Neither does the love of Christ comfort any if it is not mixed with faith, *i.e.* particularly applied to their own souls. "This is a faithful saying that Jesus Christ came into the world to save sinners, of whom I am chief," (1 Tim. 1:15). In this was the truth of the saying, that Christ came to save sinners, but the joy and comfort of Paul lay in the fact that he could say, "I am chief." It is most clear that the knowledge of the love of Christ is comforting, but the efficacy of it is in the *application*. No matter how appropriate the medication is that is prescribed by the doctor, it cannot effectively comfort or cure the patient if it is not taken. In the same way, though the knowledge of the love of Christ is the balm in Gilead which cures the sin-sick soul, it is of no benefit at all unless it is taken and particularly applied by faith. The efficacy of the right knowledge of the love of Christ to comfort in troubles is the first point of note.

Secondly, once this knowledge is rightly and particularly applied, a serious meditation on it is essential to suck out its sweetness to the heart. Application takes the medicine into the mouth and sends it down into the stomach, but the digestive processes are needed to maximize the benefit to the body. The psalmist said, "My meditation on him shall be sweet," (Psa. 104:4). Though the love of Christ is surpassingly sweet by nature, if it is not meditated on, it will not be sufficient to keep the heart from fainting. How do we appropriate the sweetness of the knowledge of this transcendent love of Christ? By remembering it and meditating on it. "We will be glad and rejoice in you, we will remember thy love more than wine," (Song of Songs 1:4).

Now let us look at how the knowledge of the love of Christ is effective in supporting the believer's soul.

First, it frees the soul from doubts and fears about its eternal condition. A great deal of virtue exists in a freedom that keeps the soul from fear of their eternal state. Even the faithful, in the midst of troubles, may show signs of fear of their eternal abode. But when that fear is removed, and that great question is resolved, they are strengthened and enabled to bear up under all their troubles.

The example of that martyr, Mr. Glover, is famous for this. He doubted his salvation for a short period of time before he suffered and died. There were many times he despaired in spirit and fainted in troubles, so that he did not find himself to be a happy man. But afterwards, when God was pleased to shine on him with the assurance of his love and to free him from this doubt, he was enabled not only to bear up under troubles, but to suffer the death of a martyr with a great deal of joy and cheerfulness.

It is easy to show how the love of Christ frees the soul from those doubts about its eternal condition. He that knows the transcendency of Christ's love will be easily freed from doubting about his condition. The knowledge of Christ's love casts out fear. And indeed, the chief ground for this doubting is the lack of the knowledge of the love of Christ. Because when the believer is able to say, "I know the love of Jesus Christ, and I know it not only for others, but myself," then he will be able to resolve anything. For why, then, should he doubt? or, who should he fear? He will think, "Seeing that Jesus Christ loves me with such a transcendent love, I am not only free from my fears, but also freed from my faintings."

Secondly, the knowledge of the love of Christ assures us of an eternal reward. If we patiently endure sufferings and tribulations, we have the promise of eternal life and happiness with our Savior. Moses did not faint in the midst of all the afflictions endured while leading the people of God out of Egypt because he was assured of the reward (Heb. 11:24-26). Notwithstanding his great tribulations, Paul was kept from fainting because he was assured of a crown of life which was laid up for him. And even Jesus Christ himself was enabled to endure the death of the cross without fainting because of the joy that was set before him (Heb. 12:2).

The knowledge of the love of Christ produces this assurance. The soul that knows how dearly Jesus Christ loves him, and what transcendent affection he has toward him, will believe that God will fully and gloriously reward him for all the tribulations he endures for him. "O!" says the believer that knows the love of Christ, "though my tribulations are many, and heavy too, yet I know I shall have a reward for all of them because Jesus loves me with a love which passes knowledge." In this way, the believer is sweetly supported from faltering.

Thirdly, a full acceptance of this rest in Christ is very effective for keeping the soul from fainting under troubles. The heart is apt to despair when it is tossed up and down. An unstable soul is like a vessel in the storm without an anchor, tossed up and down with every wave and every wind. Unstable souls are apt to fret and to faint because they do not and cannot rest in God. Hear the exhortation in Psalm 37:7, "Rest in the Lord, fret not yourself." Men fret and faint because they do not rest in the Lord. Where, if they could do the one, they would be free from the other.

The knowledge of the love of Christ brings the soul to such a resting and accepting place in Christ. When I consider how Christ loves me and how out of that love he pleads my cause for me, then am I able to rest my heart in Christ and to solace my soul in him. In this place I am so far from fainting under, or fretting at my tribulations, that I am able to patiently wait on the Lord and rejoice in him. This is how the knowledge of the love of Christ causes me to rest in him and keeps me from fainting.

Fourthly, a strength of love in the person of Jesus Christ keeps the soul from fainting under tribulations. Jacob's love for Rachel kept him from fainting under any difficulties which he endured for her. And the believer who loves Christ sufficiently is made strong by that love, strengthened to endure much for Christ without fainting. Strength of love for Christ keeps our soul from fainting under sorrow.

He that knows how transcendently Christ loves him cannot but choose to love him in return, and strongly too. O! how easily can the soul support itself from fainting under tribulations for Christ while it burns with love for him. And how easy is it for a soul not to kindle, but also enflame when it considers the transcendent love of Christ for him?

Fifthly, divine joy is forever effective in keeping the soul from fainting under trouble. There is a strengthening power in spiritual joy, and the knowledge of Christ's love produces that joy which keeps the heart from sinking under sadness.

Now you have seen in a general way the efficacy of the knowledge of Christ's love to support the spirit from fainting in times of trouble. If you could see the sum of these five things reduced into one argument, it would look like this.

If freedom from fear about a man's eternal condition... if assurance of a reward after all tribulations... if resting upon Christ in times of trouble... if strength of love to Christ and divine joy through the Spirit can keep the heart from fainting under troubles, then the knowledge of the love of Christ most certainly can because it produces all these.

But now more particularly, I shall show the *efficacy* of this knowledge to keep the heart from fainting under troubles in these four things.

First, if the knowledge of the love of Christ goes to the heart and refreshes the spirit of a believer, this same knowledge must be sufficient as it is. As the fear of God is enough to keep from us from evil, so the knowledge of the love of Christ is enough to support us from fainting under trouble because it goes to the heart and cheers the spirit. This is why Scripture uses the phrase, "shedding abroad the love of God in your hearts."

Secondly, this knowledge of the love of Christ intensifies the faculties of the soul. Paul, though mocked by the sons of Belial, did not faint because of the level of intensity of his knowledge of the love of Christ. This intense knowledge not only kept the apostle from fainting in affliction but also caused him to focus on the spiritual rewards that awaited him rather than the temporary pleasures of the world. "We look not at the things which are seen, but things which are not seen," (2 Cor. 4:16, *cf.* 18). Paul was so intensely focused on the spiritual realities of life that he did not faint at his tribulations. The contemplation of the love of Christ in the soul intensifies all its sweet dimensions. In this way the soul says which knows the love of Christ, "O the height, and depth, and length of the love of Christ! O that so great a person as Christ is should love so mean a creature as I am! O that one who is not only man, but God, should set his heart upon me, who am not only a man, but a worm!" Such intense contemplation of Christ's love keeps the soul from fainting under tribulations.

Thirdly, the knowledge of Christ's love is beneficial for making the soul forget our need to be loved by the creature. The reason we are apt to faint under tribulation is often because we put too much stock in the love of men. If we would not set our hearts so much on the love of men, we would not faint when we experience a lack of that love. They must think, "As long as I do not prize their love, nor fear their hatred, I shall never faint." The contemplation of the love of Christ *has* this effect upon the heart – it removes the need for the love and praise of men. Peter forgot the earth when he saw a glimpse of glory on the mount. Man's glory fades in the light of Christ's glory, just like the light of the stars is not seen when the light of the sun shines. And while the soul is taken with the meditation of the love of Christ which passes knowledge, he does not concern himself with the love of men.

Fourthly, the efficacy of the knowledge of Christ's love has the power to make a man forget all his tribulations. A soul that can make application and meditation of the love of Christ remembers his troubles no more. When Paul wrote this epistle, he was a prisoner at Rome. But at the same time, he was so taken with the love of Christ that he had no concern for his own troubles or imprisonment but rather prayed and poured forth his heart to the Lord on behalf of the Ephesians, that they might not faint at his tribulations or in times of trouble of their own. There is a divine, spiritual, intoxicating power in the love of Christ that causes a man not to buckle under tribulations but rather forget them. And surely the soul will never faint under that which it forgets.

We have shown you both generally, and particularly, how the power of the knowledge of the love of Christ keeps the heart from fainting under troubles. Now let's conclude with a word about application.

The point that the knowledge of Christ's love is of such special efficacy that it can keep the heart from fainting under troubles allows us to see what a great need we have to study the love of Christ. Men have much studied the nature of some plants and minerals because they are of special use for medicinal purposes. Therefore, when you know of what special use for spiritual healing the knowledge of the love of Christ is, do you not have sufficient grounds to study it? God's love met the spiritual need of man when he gave his Son, (John 3:16). Neither tribulation, nor distress, nor persecution, nor famine, nor nakedness, nor perils, nor sword can defeat the soul who knows the love of Christ. Indeed, his love is our life, (Gal. 2:20). Therefore, it is a most suitable study for the believer because it best equips him to overcome all his troubles.

Secondly, this doctrine is cause for lamentation also. How sad is it to see that though this love of Christ is so necessary and beneficial to believers in any trouble, yet they neglect it and make no use of it! They have this precious jewel in their hand and are not even aware of it or how to use it.

Another problem is that instead of using this, they use other counsels or supports in times of trouble and fail to take advantage of the knowledge of the love of Christ, which alone is able to comfort when all others fail. It is lamentable to see how believers leave this fountain of living comforts and seek after other cisterns, even broken cisterns, that neither have, nor can hold, any comfort in them.

Thirdly (which is worst of all) when Christ offers his love, they refuse to take it. How often does Christ open his heart to the believer and let him see love written in the golden letters of his free grace? How often does he implore the believer to look and live, to contemplate and take comfort from it? How often does Christ say, "Soul, I love you, I love you with an everlasting love, therefore have I drawn you into this wilderness of trouble, that here I might speak comfort to you, where none can help you?" And yet how sad it is to hear believers say that they will not believe it, though their souls might be comforted by it.

Believers, when Christ opens his heart of love to you, why will you not respond by opening your own heart widely that he may fill it with his love? Has Christ provided such a benefit for you, and you neglect it? Is there such refreshment for your souls in his love, and yet you will not use it? Does he bring it home to your hearts, and you will not take it? O you of little faith! May you be reproved for your foolishness when you will not be comforted with Christ's love.

Fourthly, allow his love to lead you in the direction you should go in time of trouble. Run to the heart of your Savior instead of going after the puddled streams of creature loves. Go instead to the running river of your Lord's love, drink of it and be refreshed and comforted in any case.

Some may ask how you may draw out the water of life that is in Christ's love? I would answer, what is the case in which you need comfort? And for what cause do you seek Christ's love? If you answer, "my case is spiritual. My soul is troubled within. I see much sin but little grace, and this goes to my heart, filling it with trouble." Believer, know that Christ loves you regardless of all this. I believe you think that Christ does not love you because your sin is so great and your grace is so little. Remember, however, though the woman at the well was a sinner, Christ's love passed by her sin and pardoned her. Christ's love took advantage of her many sins to show much love to her soul. And it is his custom, where sins abound, there to make love super-abound. Therefore, comfort yourself, sad soul, with the thoughts of Christ's love. This love made him suffer for sin, and this love makes him continue to pardon sin every day. He shows the transcendency of his love in pardoning our sin.

You might think, "But I not only have much sin; I have little grace!" It does not matter, believer. The love of Christ may comfort you regardless of your sin. You think that grace is the cause of love, but you are deceived. Grace is the effect of love. Christ does not love because there is grace; but he gives grace because he loves. Grace is given in a time of love; love is not shown because of grace. Therefore, comfort yourself at the consideration of the *transcendency* of Christ's love. It is the glory of his love that pardons much sin though there be little grace. And in time, sin will diminish, and grace will be much.

But the poor soul says, "I have lost Christ. I think there was a day in which I saw that his love was my life, and the consideration of his love was my comfort. But I have lost the one and so cannot solace myself in the other." Truly, the consideration of Christ's love may be of great benefit here. If you consider the nature of Christ's love rightly, you will know this to be the glory of it, that once had, it can never be lost. The sun may be behind a cloud so that you cannot see it. But it will appear again. The sun shall sooner leave the firmament than Christ's love shall leave you.

If you consider the transcendency of Christ's love, you will know that though Christ seems to withdraw himself for a while, yet his love will not permit his withdrawing to be long. "Yet a little while, and you shall not see me, and a little while, and you shall see me again." Christ knows your spirits would fail if he should be away for long. Because of his love, he shall never be away so long as to cause you to faint. And if you know the transcendent nature of Christ's love, you know this also. Love will come and revive you if you despair. For a moment's withdrawing it lets out everlasting kindness and departs for a season that you may have it forever.

But the soul says, "I grieve to think that I may have lost Christ through my own defect. I have been so base as to drive him out of my heart, and it pains me to think that he will never come again." Tell me why, poor soul, you are ignorant of the nature of Christ's transcendent love! If you only knew it, you would immediately resolve your grief and support it with a sweet assurance. It is the nature of transcendent love, that though you have been foolish to drive Christ away, it is so powerful that it brings Christ back again. It was the folly and the fault of the spouse, that though her beloved was knocking at her door until his locks were wet with the dew of the night, she sluggishly remained in her bed and would not let him in. Indeed, he went away that she might see her folly, but he came again that he might show love's transcendency.

But your soul says that with all this, you have violated and wronged the beautiful love that exists between Christ and his bride; and these thoughts sink your spirit, for fear that Christ will not overlook this.

I say still, believer, that if you but understood the nature of the transcendent love of Christ, it would offer you assurance in this case also. This is the glory of this love; it forgives such violations. The love of men does not, but the love of Christ forgives foul transgressions because Christ's love transcends men's love. Christ's word to his people was, "You have played the harlot with many lovers, yet return to me," (Jer. 3:1). "Surely," (God says), "as a wife treacherously departs from her husband, so have you dealt with me, O house of Israel, yet return you backsliding people, and I will heal your backslidings." What transcendent love! Observe the love in Christ's heart which *pardons* even the defilement of the bed of love. Indeed, there is no failing so great. If you know and understand the transcendency of Christ's love, you would see that it is greater than any failing of your own, so that now in case this fear should disturb your assurance, yet the consideration of Christ's love may support your soul and bring comfort to you.

You say, "Yet I hear others cry out, and say, how shall we draw out joy from this well of salvation? How shall we make the consideration of Christ's love a comfort to us in our troubles?" What are your troubles that make you stand in need of the comfort of this consideration? Even if you have lost all for the sake of Christ's love, it will still comfort you during your loss. It is the nature of transcendent love to repair all losses, and even restore double, (Isa. 61:17). And there is no man that has left parents, brethren, house, or children for Christ, but love will make up for it all, (Luke 18:29). Allow this truth to comfort you.

Another may say, "I have not only lost all, but am still opposed; they have stripped me of everything for Christ's sake and threaten my very life. How shall I comfort myself with the consideration of Christ's love now?"

Consider that Christ will comfort at the same time as men oppose. Transcendent love gives the soul consolation in any tribulation in which you find yourself. "In the world you shall have tribulation," (Christ says), "but be of good cheer, I have overcome the world, and in me you shall have peace." Transcendent love gives a smile for every frown, a kiss for every suffering, an embrace for every blow. This is the nature of his love, so be of good comfort.

Consider that even in death, Christ's love has provided a comfort. For you shall have your life by losing it. If you die for him, you will secure your life. "Because I live, you shall live also," (John 14:19). Being absent from the body is to be immediately present with the Lord. In but a wink of the eye, and you enter the land of eternity.

The place to go for comfort in any tribulation is to Christ's heart, and there you will find in his love a comforting assurance in any tribulations, whether within or without, spiritual or corporal. Be directed on all occasions, believers, to run to Christ's love and to comfort yourselves in the consideration of it.

If you do not belong to Christ, then to hear that Christ's love will support you in any trouble is of no benefit. Sinners have no right to his love, for tribulation is a just reward for every soul that sins, (Rom. 2:9). You will meet with tribulation, Christless creatures; ere long, divine wrath will come and visit you. What will you do in the day of God's wrath? Where will you run for consolation in the hour of your trouble? Will you run to men? Miserable comforters they will be. Men of high degree are vanity, and men of low degree are a lie. Where can you go when your soul anguishes? Will you run to your duties? They will do you no good, for without Christ they are worthless. Will you say you are in Christ? The Scriptures will refute you, for the Bible says, "if any be in Christ, he is a new creature," (2 Cor. 5:17). Do not say, "I am baptized," for many are baptized into Christ's name who are not baptized into his person and therefore have no right to Christ.

Tremble, therefore, you Christless creatures, for you have no part in his love. What will become of you when Christ appears in wrath? It will do you no good to call to the mountains to hide you from the wrath of the lamb. Nothing, nothing will be able to support your souls. When he appears in flames of fire, believers will be able to comfort themselves with the knowledge of his transcendent love; but alas, you who have no right to Christ, what will you do in that day? If you remain as you are, you will doubtless sink in despair and die under his wrath.

Inasmuch as the knowledge of the love of Christ is of such special efficacy to support your souls under tribulations, then be exhorted, my fellow believers to labor to be well acquainted with the love of Christ in its substance, its circumstances, and especially in its fullness and freeness. Read, study, pray, do what you can, that you may be acquainted with this love – the knowledge and consideration of which is a comfort in any trouble.

Secondly, labor to assure yourselves that you have a share in this love and a right to it. Especially strive to see that though you once had no part in it because you were born *children of wrath* without Christ, yet now because you have been *born again* by the Lord Christ, you have a share in that transcendent love which is in him.

Thirdly, on all occasions run to this fountain of love. Draw out of it the necessary comforts and healing for any of your troubles. In all occasions, labor that the love of Christ may keep your spirits from fainting.

Consider what times you are in and when you may expect to meet with tribulation. I cannot assure you that you will receive comfort from the world; neither can I assure you of kind dealings from those who call themselves Christian. But this I can assure you, if on the words of grace you act in faith and come to Christ, he will certainly sweeten your troubles.

You have heard that there is love in his heart for every believer, and that love is of a transcendent nature. You have also heard how that it concerns you all to labor and study for the knowledge of it. And now you hear that if you attain its right spiritual knowledge, it will be very comforting to you in any trouble.

I implore you, therefore, as you prize your souls, as you prize comfort in tribulations, believe, and labor to get a part in Christ; and then know that no matter what your condition may be, or whether the world shall go well or ill with you, you shall still find a friend in Christ. He will still follow you with a full, free, comforting, and transcendent love.

So finally, let the consideration of the love that is in Christ to believers, and of all the comfort that is in that love in any troubles, prevail with you to look after it and to lay hold upon Jesus Christ. Then shall you know experientially that the love of Christ passes knowledge.

FINIS

Other Helpful Works Published by Puritan Publications

A Call to Delaying Sinners
by Thomas Doolittle (1632–1707)

A Treatise of the Loves of Christ to His Spouse
by Samuel Bolton, D.D. (1606-1654)

Attending the Lord's Table
by Henry Tozer (1602-1650)

Faith, Election and the Believer's Assurance
by George Gifford (1547-1620)

God is Our Refuge and Our Strength
by George Gipps (n.d.)

Remembering Your Creator
by Matthew Mead (1630-1699)

Resisting the Devil with a Steadfast Faith
by George Gifford (1547-1620)

Taking Hold of Eternal Life in Christ
by George Gifford (1547-1620)

The Believer's Marriage with Christ
by Michael Harrison (1640-1729)

The Doctrine of Man's Future Eternity
by John Jackson (1600-1648)

The Victorious Christian Soldier in Christ's Army
by Urian Oakes (1631–1681)

Zeal for God's House Quickened
by Oliver Bowles B.D. (1574-1664?)

The Five Principles of the Gospel
by C. Matthew McMahon

The Excellent Name of God
by Jeremiah Burroughs (1599-1646)

The Blessed God
by Daniel Burgess (1645-1713)

John 3:16 (2nd Edition)
by C. Matthew McMahon

www.ingramcontent.com/pod-product-compliance
Lightning Source LLC
Chambersburg PA
CBHW051428090426
42737CB00014B/2860

* 9 7 8 1 6 2 6 6 3 3 9 9 5 *